T0368226

TOO BIG
FOR SMALL THINGS,
TOO SMALL FOR
BIG THINGS

*Unveiling the
mysteries and
mechanics behind
ascending to the top
and staying humble
while there*

PAULINE KANGE

WESTBOW
P R E S S®
A DIVISION OF THOMAS NELSON
& ZONDERVAN

WestBow Press books may be ordered through booksellers or by contacting:

WestBow Press
A Division of Thomas Nelson & Zondervan
1663 Liberty Drive
Bloomington, IN 47403
www.westbowpress.com
1 (866) 928-1240

Unless marked otherwise, all Scripture quotations are taken from the King James Version.

Scripture quotations marked AMP are taken from the Amplified® Bible, Copyright © 2015 by The Lockman Foundation. Used by permission.

Scripture quotations marked "Aramaic Bible in Plain English" are taken from The Original Aramaic New Testament in Plain English- with Psalms & Proverbs Copyright © 2007; 8th edition Copyright © 2013. All rights reserved. Used by Permission.

Scripture quotations marked DRA are taken from the Douay-Rheims Bible.

Scripture quotations marked NLT are taken from the Holy Bible, New Living Translation, Copyright © 1996, 2004, 2015 by Tyndale House Foundation. Used by permission of Tyndale House Publishers, Inc., Carol Stream, Illinois 60188. All rights reserved.

ISBN: 978-1-9736-8807-5 (sc)
ISBN: 978-1-9736-8808-2 (hc)
ISBN: 978-1-9736-8806-8 (e)

Library of Congress Control Number: 2020904613

Print information available on the last page.

WestBow Press rev. date: 05/23/2024

Too Big for Small Things, Too Small for Big Things provokes thoughts that will generate self-examination and bring about behavior modification at the core of one's being. Change that is superficial, lip service, and meant just to impress or gain a few dollars is exactly that—superficial.

—Dr. Peter Kange, Senior Pastor, Reaching the Nations Ministries International, Beltsville, MD

To my sons and daughters.

Contents

Part I
Diligence and Accountability

Part II
Listen! Service Is Speaking

Foreword

In these times and seasons in which success and achievement sell so high, days in which money seems to answer all things and the world is more about the haves and hardly about the have-nots, the conversation has never been any timelier. *Too Big for Small Things, Too Small for Big Things* provokes thoughts that will generate self-examination and bring about behavior modification at the core of one's being. Change that is superficial, lip service, and meant just to impress or gain a few dollars, is exactly that—superficial. It is hardly common experience to come across the information in this book. Reading through, one comes to an absolute conclusion that protocol has nothing to do with wrong or right or evil or good but rather an acceptable, existing, and established pattern of life within a particular institution, realm, or environment. Anyone who does not follow from a place of honor, the protocol of achievement, will not attain success. When you choose to enter an environment or platform, it becomes your duty to study the ethics in order to not only gain access but also to maintain your stay. If you ascend to a platform for which you did not pay the price to access, either because someone put in a good word for you or by inheritance as in birthright, chances are you will drop for failure to accomplish your due diligence in doing what is necessary to stay there. The world is full of opportunities to serve and be served. So, pay attention!

—Dr. Peter Kange, President and CEO,
The Diamond Network Group

Acknowledgments

I acknowledge my Lord and Savior Jesus Christ, my reason for living; my husband and friend, Peter Kange; and my Reaching the Nations Ministries family. Thanks for all you do. Jehovah rewards!

Introduction

> If you are too big for small things, then
> you are too small for big things!

My pastor, the late Ruth Dione Alangeh, regularly mentioned the above statement whenever she talked about one of the fundamental principles underlining growth and increase. As the years have gone by, it has become clearer how profoundly scriptural and pivotal that statement is. Jesus's entire life and ministry were all about service unto the Father by serving the people. He demonstrated this kingdom principle by washing the feet of His disciples:

> Jesus knowing that the Father had given all things into his hands, and that he was come from God, and went to God; He riseth from supper, and laid aside his garments; and took a towel, and girded himself. After that he poureth water into a bason, and began to wash the disciples' feet, and to wipe them with the towel wherewith he was girded. Then cometh he to Simon Peter: and Peter saith unto him, Lord, dost thou wash my feet? (John 13:3–6)

Ye call me Master and Lord: and ye say well; for so I am. If I then, your Lord and Master, have washed your feet; ye also ought to wash one another's feet. For I have given you an example, that ye should do as I have done to you (John 13:13–15)

On another occasion, He gave an expository sermon to convey the same message. Placing a child in the midst of His disciples, He contrasted the world's system of success and achievement with the kingdom's: "Anyone who is great among you," He said, "must be your minister" (Matthew 18:1–4). In other words, the way up is the way down.

Many are looking for preaching engagements and connections to big ministers and their ministries, with the intention of becoming famous and popular. Unfortunately, they think that fame and popularity are achieved by passing out business cards and having someone put in a good word for them to the people they are trying to impress. On the contrary, God's kingdom module presents a dual drive and mind-set depicting the minister as the one serving, rather than the one served, and every performed act of service is unto the Lord. It makes perfect sense that the word minister actually means servant. We can trace everyone in scripture who has ever played a strategic role in their world to a moment of service. When you stop serving, you start to dry out. When you stop serving, you start dying. In your current daily service is found the guarantee of your future greatness.

There are faceless and nameless people doing great things for God through the ministry of helps. These are those who come in early and leave late; they set up before everyone else arrives and break down after everyone leaves. They clean toilets and restrooms, vacuum floors, wash pots, handle trash, arrange sound, assist with children, and take care of audiovisual needs, ushering, transportation, home visits for the sick and shut-ins, and more. These are the people who God is strategically positioning for the end-time harvest. God told us that the end-time revival would be a resurgence of positioning within its core, and those who will heed His call to take off their jackets, roll back their sleeves, and take hold of a pruning hook and plowshare without being afraid of dirt are those He is willing to use.

There were seven men chosen in Acts 6:1–6 to serve tables (food distribution) who began experiencing a move of the Spirit, among whom were Philip and Stephen. Throughout the Bible, we see stories of ordinary men and women who served with no hidden agenda and no motive for climbing the ladder. They did not even know there was any ladder to climb; they just served God in different capacities as the need arose.

> Who (with reason) despises the day of small things (beginnings)? (Zechariah 4:10 AMP)

> Though thy beginning was small, yet thy latter end should greatly increase. (Job 8:7)

> A little one shall become a thousand and a small one a strong nation: I the LORD will hasten it in his time. (Isaiah 60:22)

A project that looks small, or a church that is considered miniature, or a business that seems inconsiderable does not indicate failure. In a society where success is equivalent to size, the church world has to be very cautious not to lose its foresight into God's mind-set and principles. Many have been quick to judge and conclude that your business may not have been God's will because it is small, or that the Holy Spirit has left your ministry because of the size of its membership. God, however, uses these measurements to analyze motives because **mind-set determines success**. If you despise the day of small beginnings, there will never be a big day for your project or business or church. Though your starting point is small, God promises a great increase in the latter end, if you do not despise small beginnings. Lack of diligence is an indication of an existing spite for the small beginnings.

Seest thou a man diligent in his business? He shall stand before kings; he shall not stand before mean men. (Proverbs 22:29)

PART I
DILIGENCE AND ACCOUNTABILITY

The storms of life will cause you to either quit or soar.
Diligence and accountability will enable you break
through life's challenges, into your next level of success.
Stay diligent and be accountable. No quitting!

1

Diligence: The Secret Weapon

Diligent: constant and earnest in effort and application;
attentive and persistent in doing something.
—Dictionary.com

A faithful, hardworking person shall access greatness because God rewards faithfulness with greater responsibilities. Consistency over a period of time constitutes diligence or devotion. There is no valid instrument with which to measure diligence or faithfulness without the variables of consistency and time. The mathematical equation for such a concept would be as follows: Consistency x Time = Diligence.

You must have done something continuously over time for someone to consider you faithful or diligent. A sagacious king once said that he who deals with a slack and idle hand would become poor, but the hand of the diligent makes rich (Proverbs 10:4 AMP, paraphrased). This suggests that the riches were only evident over a given period. Diligence in knowing the state of your flock, as a pastor, will produce for you consistent and stable people with whom to establish a discipleship cycle. Adequate care of the flock will create a system of multiplication and increase, providing food for your household, milk, clothing, and maintenance of your maids (Proverbs 27:23–27AMP).

Apostle Paul counsels Timothy, his son in the faith, to commit the things he heard from him to faithful men, who shall be able to teach others.

> And the things that thou hast heard of me among many witnesses, the same commit thou to faithful men, who shall be able to teach others also. (2 Timothy 2:2)

In Paul's advice to Timothy, the secret to duplicity and talent mastery is repetition. At the onset of mentoring, the outcome is not apparent, yet with consistency, over time, there will be a formation of the intended mission. Timothy's task was to make sure he committed what he had learned from Paul to faithful men. Not only does it require due diligence to identify committed people, but it also demands consistency over time to deposit within them what you have become by learning. It takes commitment to commit because the investment passed on has a tendency to be slippery and nonsticky. If you are to transfer learned behavior successfully, you must primarily be a lover of repetition in order to get such material to stick.

Second, Timothy is to commit what he has learned from Paul. If you are not teachable, you are unable to teach, regardless of how much knowledge you have. If you cannot humble yourself to learn, you are not qualified to teach. Most successful CEOs will tell you how much they learned from their employees, which led to their success.

When you have proven yourself faithful by your ability to learn from someone else, you are entrusted with the responsibility to teach and multiply yourself in other reliable people. That is the kingdom module of discipleship that runs all successful industries in the world. Someone must supervise you before you can be positioned to monitor others, hence the orientation required for every hired employee. I have experienced my fair share in the workplace, dealing with different people assigned to my training as well as those I had to orient. When you have had a bad experience, it teaches you what not to do to someone else in your shoes—hopefully! Were you ever oriented at a job by someone who told you how they cut corners to get the basics done, without actually telling you what the company expected as its mode of operation? People like that train you to be mediocre because they have concluded that you have no prospects for growth within that company. Don't fall for the bait. Learn the right things the right way. Some people are kind enough to tell you how the company wants the tasks done and then show you how they get it done. You have to use your discretion and excellent work ethic to determine the right thing to do.

In his letter to the Corinthians, regarding their preparation of offerings to be collected, Paul says, "We sent our brother, whom we have often proved diligent in many things" (2 Corinthians 8:22). They could trust him with the offering contributions because of his testimony of diligence in other matters. This brother's diligence was up to the test—unbeknown to him, I suppose! And they found him trustworthy. Do you know that people are watching you daily? Can you be trusted with money? There are people in your world, with the ability to promote you, who have been testing your diligence without your knowledge. Be trustworthy!

> He that is faithful in that which is least is faithful also in much: and he that is unjust in the least is unjust also in much.
>
> If therefore ye have not been faithful in the unrighteous mammon, who will commit to your trust the true riches?
>
> And if ye have not been faithful in that which is another man's, who shall give you that which is your own? (Luke 16:10–12)

Jesus speaks explicitly of this fundamental principle: he who is faithful in that which is least is faithful also in that which is much, and he who is unjust in that which is least is unjust in that which is much. If you have a hard time tithing off $1,000, you will have a significant difficulty tithing off $1 million. If you cannot consistently take care of three children in the kids' church, you will be unable to handle fifteen children in the same scenario. Ineffective management of a $5,000 inventory business will become a hindrance to your growth to $10,000. The servant who did not make proper use of his talent did not get more; on the contrary, even that which he had was taken away from him. But those who multiplied theirs were made rulers over many things (Matthew 25:14–28).

Jesus asks a mind-boggling question in verse 11 of Luke 16. "If you have not been faithful in the unrighteous mammon, who will commit to your trust the true riches?" So the money test (faithfulness in tithes and offerings, charitable giving, and financial management) is not about money. It is a diligence test to determine your ability to handle and manage the true riches of the anointing. Can you quickly release money at God's command? Are you faithful with your finances by following the kingdom's financial principles?

As a copastor and cofounder of a ministry, I know what it means to stretch a dollar to do the impossible. Some years ago, we believed God would provide a venue to have church services, so we fasted and prayed for it. At about the same time, we were invited to a revival service at another church on a Friday night. Considering my schedule, it was a little challenging because we had only one car at the time. The only remedy was for my husband to drive and pick me up from work, which he gladly did. However, that meant I had to change my clothes in the car and freshen up in the church bathroom to avoid tardiness (especially knowing that out of respect for clergy, they might take us all the way to a front seat). With that job, employees got paid weekly on Fridays at the close of business, but suppose you got paid directly into your account and the payment came in Thursday night into Friday. I had just collected my weekly pay and set aside my first 10 percent as the tithe.

While at the service that evening, the preacher called for a particular offering intended for the building fund. I heard the still, small voice that speaks to all of us say, "Give everything you have." Following this intuitive instruction, I engaged in forcing and fighting with what I very well knew was God. I decided to put everything I got from the paycheck into that offering basket, almost in tears. "God, You see this is all the money we have! Why do I have to give it here? Why didn't You tell me to give it to our building fund? I hope You know we need it more than they do, given the fact that their church membership is way bigger than ours. What will my husband say when I tell him that I just gave away all the money we were looking forward to using for the week ahead of us?"

Oh! Did I mention that I did not discuss it with him before giving the money? He was at the opposite corner of the room, playing the keyboard for the offering song. Yes, exactly!

All these thoughts and questions were flying through my head when I heard that voice again. "That's not all," He said.

Looking perplexed, I said, "I don't understand. I gave everything."

Then He said, "In the car."

I ran out to the car, opened the compartments, and pulled out all the change I could find. I felt so embarrassed at the sound it made when it hit the offering bucket. Despite the logical embarrassment and analysis going on in my head, I felt a surge of joy and contentment within, with a gentle assurance that we were going to be okay. I felt honored that God could use our little amount to meet the need in His kingdom, and I was especially grateful that His grace enabled me to obey, despite my internal struggles.

Needless to say, God miraculously provided a church location for us, and I have grown to release more easily whatever God demands. I have equally grown, by His grace, in my awareness of the truth that He owns everything in my possession, and it is an honor to be counted as a good steward. It is a heart test, not a money test. If you are not faithful with money, you will not be faithful with the anointing.

What is Jesus saying?

If you misuse finances, you will misuse the anointing.

If money is used to manipulate and control people, the same tendency will develop with the utilization of the anointing to manipulate and control people.

If you cheat the system and cut corners to get money, you will try to cut corners and do unscriptural things for the anointing.

The anointing is a tool of exchange in the realm of the spirit, as money is in the visible world system. Both are tools of power, so wield them for kingdom purposes only. Make sure you have money and money doesn't have you; then make sure that God has both you and your money. When the rich young ruler could not release his finances as Jesus instructed him to do, Jesus said, "How hard it is for those who trust in riches to enter the Kingdom of God!" (Mark 10:24).

Jesus takes this Luke 16 discourse a step further when he asks another question in verse 12: If you have not been faithful with that which is another man's, who shall give you that which is your own? Many people want to start their own business, build their own ministry, raise their own family, have their individual home, and the list goes on. All these desires are great and godly, but if you do not sow positive seeds in the way you handle someone else's business, there will be a problem with yours when the time comes. If all you do now is criticize your pastor and church, talking about how you will do things differently when you start your personal ministry, you will not go far. If you cannot take out the trash, clean the bathroom, and wash the dishes in your parents' or someone else's home, your personal home will be a dump. That is, if you ever get to cheat your way into having yours.

No one can cheat the laws of the universe, even though it sometimes looks as if some do. The Holy Bible says, "God cannot be mocked. Whatever a man sows, that shall he also reap" (Galatians 6:7). God uses the small things to test and measure our ability to handle and manage greatness. If you cannot deal with a toilet brush or a vacuum cleaner because you think you are too big for those kinds of assignments, then your hands are not qualified to handle a microphone and are certainly not fit to be laid on anyone. Watch out how you look down on daily menial tasks that do not require flamboyance. Those so-called menial jobs make up the tools that build one into greatness.

If you are too big to sit down and receive when someone else is teaching, you are too small to teach.

If you are too big for backup singing, you are too small for a lead role in music.

"If you are too big for small things, then you are too small for big things!"

2 Accountability Births Responsibility

The greatest teacher that ever lived used parables about practical, daily events to communicate profound divine and eternal truths. In Luke 16:1-2, Jesus gave a parable about a rich man who had a steward accused of wasting his master's goods. The rich man called him and demanded that he provide an account of his stewardship, without which he would be relieved of his duties as his steward. In other words, if he did not present proper and satisfactory accounts, he would be fired.

For you to access a certain level of greatness and success in anything you do, you must learn accountability. You must be accountable to the one who is master over you for your stewardship to be profitable and consequently rewarded. Your boss expects reports on his desk either daily or weekly, and you know your retaining that position is dependent on your efficiency. Documentation is paramount as a form of accountability in all walks of life. In the nursing field, we are often told, "If it was not documented, it was not done." Your documentation or accountability is likely to have a profound effect on your work quality. You will lose your job or your position in that organization if you think you can do whatever you please and give no account of your activities.

Every employee has a supervisor; every pastor has a pastor (or should have one); every CEO is answerable to a board; every organization has a supervisory position handled by agency rules and regulations, which makes them accountable and keeps them in check. There is always a system of checks and balances in place, with the intention of providing guidelines for appropriate and acceptable behavior or code of conduct. It is very dangerous for anyone to become so big and powerful that they answer to no one. That lack of accountability is a recipe for disaster. If you surround yourself with a bunch of yes-men for friends, and you have no revered mentor, you will find yourself in a ditch. You need to have people (or at least someone) who can look at you squarely in the face and tell you when you are acting stupid. I heard Dr. Mike Murdock say we are always doing something stupid, and it's just a matter of when you find out. I also heard Les Brown say, "You can't see the picture when you are in the frame." Be intentional about your accountability. It will save your life. Be accountable to your supervisor, your spouse, your pastor, your coach, your leader, or whatever authority is present in your life and world.

You may have heard stories of people who were discovered a week or two after they died in their homes. That is totally outrageous! In some cases, maybe the neighbor said, "He always tells me when he is going out of town, and he comes home from work around six o'clock every day. This is strange, and I think something is wrong." I remember an incident where a member of the church did not come home one day after work. His brother called me and said something was wrong because this brother was very accountable in everything. If he had other errands to run, he would call home to let them know that he would not be heading home directly after work. Someone always knew where he was and what he was doing. We immediately rallied the office staff and began making calls to extended family and friends (which were not many) and then hospitals. After hours of phone calls with no sign of him, we reluctantly started calling detention centers. It was not yet twenty-four hours, so we knew we could not file a missing person report just yet. But we were convinced that something was wrong because of his lifestyle of accountability. We were able to locate him in jail finally, and God did a beautiful miracle toward his release. Praise God! Parents have received shocking news of their child being in an accident in North Carolina when the child was supposed to have been in class at the University of Maryland. I read a joke on Facebook in which a married man did not know how to come back home after lying to his wife that he was going on a business trip; he was supposedly on the plane that crashed with no survivors. Be authentically accountable.

Accountability creates a platform for feedback, which determines growth. When Jesus sent out his twelve disciples with instructions to heal the sick and preach the kingdom, among other things, they returned with reports (Luke 9:1–10). When He sent out the seventy, they also returned with joy, recounting how demons were subject to them (Luke 10:1, 17). Jesus had the opportunity to redirect their misconstrued perspective and focus by telling them what the right reason for rejoicing should be—that their "names are written" (Luke 10:19–20). Without accountability, they would have been a bunch of boastful, self-exalted disciples more focused on their ability to cast out demons than the grace of God at work within them, which guaranteed their salvation.

After finishing my Bible training, I returned to our ministry for some practical work and lived on the ministry grounds. My late pastor was a shepherd to ministers, and she always drilled into us the consciousness of ministry. She assigned me to a demon-possessed case that needed physical healing. In similar situations, she expected me to hear God, decipher the problem, and follow the Holy Spirit's leading to determine the course of action. As a result, she just mentioned the condition presented by the lady, and told me to go handle it. By the very visible hand of God, she was delivered and healed instantly as the demons manifested and left her body. I was elated and super excited, of course, as I gave reports to my pastor later on. I did not realize the extent to which I was pumped up with pride in the story of how I prayed and the demons left. My loving and very stern pastor patiently waited for me to finish rambling. She had a tendency of developing a darker shade in her complexion around the eyelids when she was going to say something quite intense. With those perforating eyes, she gently yet firmly looked me straight in the eyes and said: "Do you realize that this woman could have been you but for the grace of God?" That question sliced through that balloon of pride and took all the air out of it instantly! I will forever be grateful for that moment moving forward. It marked me for life. Every time God saves, heals, delivers, or comes through for a person in any way using me, I remember that it could have been me, if not of God's grace. I can still see my pastor's face as she stood talking to me. It humbles me and makes me genuinely grateful and honored to be used by God. When you are accountable, you give access to correction and growth. In the multitude of counselors there is safety, and by wise counsel, you can wage your war (Proverbs 24:6).

I was watching Christian television one day and heard this preacher yell, "You can choose to learn by mentorship or mistakes!" I am not entirely sure if he actually yelled or if God just magnified the sound of it to get my attention. He definitely achieved the goal. He got my attention!

Your decision and accountable action positions you for the acquisition of knowledge by mentorship, sparing you the pain of errors and time wasted. If the steward with the one talent had built a lifestyle of accountability, he would have received counsel that burying his lord's money was not such a good idea. He learned a very powerful lesson and a principle of life: if you do not multiply your resources, you'll lose them. Unfortunately, he learned it through the pain of error and wasting time (Mathew 25:26–29). Since he was too big (in his own eyes) to be accountable, he was considered too small for responsibility. The one talent was taken away from him and given to the one who had multiplied his talents.

Saul lost his position and authority as king over Israel because of lack of accountability to Samuel the prophet. He refused to follow the instructions given by God through the prophet but rather lied and made it about the people when he was required to be accountable (1 Samuel 15:23, 26). The sons of Eli perverted the house of God and made a mockery of God's holy altar. God sent a man to tell priest Eli that He had withdrawn His promise of unending priesthood because of their lack of accountability to His requirements. He was going to eliminate them from the priesthood position and raise for Himself a faithful priest (1 Samuel 2:27–36). They acted as though they were too big for accountability, and God took away their position of responsibility as priests. Queen Vashti publicly defied the instructions of the king and humiliated him by sending word of her disobedience through his chamberlains. The king sought counsel from his wise men, who told him that if he did not make a public example of the queen, all the women would despise their husbands. Queen Vashti lost her position as queen because she thought that obeying the king's command was beneath her. Because she felt too big to follow the king's command, she was declared too small to remain queen (Esther 1:10–22).

Proper accountability helps you determine prayer direction and battle strategy. The book of Acts, which is a prototype of the New Testament church of Jesus Christ, shows us the lifestyle of the apostles and believers. When they were arrested and beaten, they returned to their own company and gave reports (Acts 4:23–24). Their accountability determined their prayer direction and battle strategy for the future. As a person in a decision-making position, you are faced very often with situations where you have to depend on the reports of others to make the right judgment call. The CEO's decision-making can sometimes depend on the departmental reports of the managers. If their reports are faulty, that CEO could make a major decision error, based on the wrong information. Barnabas's respect and sense of accountability toward the apostles gave Saul a platform and acceptance among the believers whom he had previously persecuted (Acts 9:26–28). They might have feared and avoided Saul much longer if Barnabas had not given those reports of Saul's conversion experience.

In certain families, there are seasonal occurrences at certain times of the year. These are mostly tragic events such as deaths, accidents, illness, and so on, which indicate the presence of curses. Every curse has a cause or reason for being (Proverbs 26:2). Such curses that are only noticeable after a while bring about a measure of uncertainty toward their demolition. Curses can be easily broken through prayers once the causes are identified and the rules of engagement are accurately appropriated to ensure freedom. If you do your homework in prayer and fasting and you talk to elderly family members about your lineage, you will discover information that will enable you to fight right and tackle the problem at its source. Without this strategy, you will be cutting the branches but not uprooting the stump. We had a similar story in my family, but once the root(cause) was identified, we revised the battle strategy, and victory was ours. It could be yours as well.

Accountability brings clarity and determines the course of action. The apostles demanded an explanation from Peter after they heard that he went in and fellowshipped with Gentiles. Some of the believers were hostile toward him, opposing and disputing and contending with him (Acts 11:2 Amplified) because he had eaten with the uncircumcised. Peter was humble and respectful of the apostles as he explained everything that took place from the beginning to the end. He did not say the other apostles had no right to question his actions (though he was equally an apostle) but was ready to rehearse everything as the Holy Ghost had orchestrated it (Acts 11:1–4). When they heard Peter's account, fresh discretion and illumination emerged, which determined their future course of action, as they now realized God's working in the midst of Gentile nations (Acts 11:8). After Peter's miraculous release from jail, he recounted the events to the brethren that were at Mary's house. He further instructed them to tell "James and the brethren," because he had to depart to another place after the prison break (Acts 12:17). The rest of the brethren would not have known of his release from jail if Peter had not been accountable. In Acts 13:1–4, the apostles obeyed the voice of the Holy Ghost, prayed, and released Barnabas and Saul for missions. When they returned from their missionary journey, they gave reports to leadership (Acts 14:26–28).

Accountability sets a trend of transparency, leaving no room for assumptions and misunderstanding. The enemy cannot succeed in sowing seeds of discord among people who understand the power of accountability and use it. Barnabas and Paul (formerly Saul) faced difficulties with certain Jewish believers who insisted that the Gentiles must be circumcised to be saved. To resolve this problem, Barnabas and Paul returned to Jerusalem to seek counsel from the apostles and elders. After careful deliberations and examination of the acts of the Holy Ghost amongst the Gentiles, as recounted by Barnabas and Paul, James spoke, quoting other accounts given to him by other believers. They concluded that circumcision was an unnecessary burden to lay upon the gentiles, as it seemed good to the Holy Ghost and them, and sent out letters to the churches, restoring joy and consolation (Acts 15:1–31). The churches were established because there was accountability, which brought clarity and direction (Acts 16:4–5). The writer of the book of Hebrews urges us not to forget to be accountable to those in authority over us, knowing that they watch for our souls as ones that must also give account (Hebrews 13:16–17). Be accountable, even as you expect those under you to be, being mindful of the Chief Shepherd above all (1 Peter 5:2–4). Your accountability determines your level of responsibility. If you are too big for accountability, you are undoubtedly too small for responsibility.

PART II

LISTEN! SERVICE IS SPEAKING

Service has a voice and a message. Every time you serve,
you are saying something. The Bible is full of examples
of people in service whose actions spoke distinctly and
continue to speak. Significant and strategic people
in scripture were found in a place of service.

3 The Language and Disposition of service

—Abigail (1 Samuel 25)

S he was a woman of good understanding and of beautiful countenance, but her husband, Nabal, was rough and evil in his doings (verse 3). David and his men had been pleasant to Nabal's servants in the fields, and they hoped Nabal would show the same generosity when they were in need of food supplies. When Nabal refused to assist them and was boldly disrespectful in his approach, David decided to retaliate by killing every male thing in Nabal's house (verses 10–13, 21, 22). One of Nabal's servants reported to Abigail how Nabal had audaciously turned down David and his men. He went on further to give an account of these people's help extended toward them while they were in the field (verses 14–16). This servant then cautioned Abigail to consider what necessary action to take, bearing in mind that her husband was "such a man of Belial that a man cannot speak to him" (verse 17).

It is evil to have the kind of disposition that provides no room for anyone to talk to you. Having an unteachable, know-it-all attitude will shut the door to your deliverance and put your family in danger. Are you known as someone who never listens? Do you have a pattern of always giving excuses or explanations when anyone points out a character flaw in you? You shut out wise and life-saving counsel when you need it the most because people around you know that you will not listen. Keep communication doors open by appreciating the feedback, even if you think it is not valuable or meaningful. A teachable disposition will save your life. Contrary to Nabal, his wife had a nature of service, which made her very approachable to her servants. Valuable information came to her knowledge through a servant, and she immediately went to work. Abigail is portrayed as a woman with great insight and incredible speed.

- She made haste to prepare food fit to serve a king and his entourage (verse 18). How quick are you to be hospitable? We see this same type of haste with Abraham in Genesis 18:1–14 when he constrained three men to eat at his house. They prophesied the birth of Isaac after they ate, and it turned out that Abraham had entertained angels without knowing. Paul admonishes the believer to be one that is given to hospitality (Romans 12:13). We are told that many have entertained angels unawares because of their hospitable disposition (Hebrews 13:2).

- She made haste to get off the donkey and bow before David when she approached him (verse 23). How quickly do you discern greatness? How quickly do you respond to greatness by honor? Give honor to whom it is due. Recognize and honor those who have gone ahead of you and have made major contributions to the fabric of society in a way that brings impact. You cannot receive from that which you do not honor.

- She made haste to apologize for the faults of her husband, taking the blame for his churlish behavior. She was not trying to impress the future king at her husband's expense; she was seeking to save her family and servants. Abigail demonstrated the team concept of sharing the blame and not passing the buck (verse 28). Are you one who partakes in the victories but dishes out blame? Are you a team player?

- She understood the urgency and importance of her service. David testifies that if she had not made haste, he would have killed every male in Nabal's house.

- Her intercessory disposition made her own the faults of the one for whom she was interceding. She stood in the gap for the men in her household and convinced the king to repent of his plans against Nabal's house. Her language of service melted David's heart, as she constantly referred to herself as his handmaiden.

- After Nabal died, King David took Abigail as his wife. Her language and disposition of service brought her royal attention and position. She intrigued David so much that day that she left an imprint in him. She became unforgettable.

- Abigail remained a servant even after she knew she had become King David's wife. She offered to wash the feet of King David's servants that came for her (verses

40–41). When you have a heart and disposition of service, position and greatness will locate you but will not change you. The actions and resolutions that made you access prominence are the same elements that will sustain and maintain you on that platform.

Never stop doing what you did to obtain greatness; diligence brings you before kings and will keep you at the top. Refuse to become puffed up after attaining a position of power or fame. The Shunammite woman was a lady of great substance, but her language was that of service (2 Kings 4:8–10), as evidenced in the way she constrained Elisha to eat bread at her house. Lydia was an influential woman who traded in purple, yet her language reflected service as she constrained Paul and others to stay in her house (Acts 16:14–15). These women did not use their position and status to become bossy or demanding; neither did they demonstrate any sense of entitlement. They manifested a disposition and language of service and counted it a privilege to be granted access to serve. Refuse to walk in pride and arrogance. When God positions you to serve His people in whatever capacity, consider it a privilege and cherish it as such.

> Having then gifts differing according to the grace that is given to us, whether prophecy, let us prophesy according to the proportion of faith;
>
> Or ministry, let us wait on our ministering: or he that teacheth, on teaching;

Or he that exhorteth, on exhortation: he that giveth, let him do it with simplicity; he that ruleth, with diligence; he that sheweth mercy, with cheerfulness. (Romans 12:6–8)

When you give, is it done simply? Are you grateful for the opportunity to sow in the life of God's child? Or does your ability to give cause you to walk with a sense of superiority? When you understand that your service of hospitality brings blessings to you, your attitude in this service will shift. The Shunammite's hospitality to Elisha removed barrenness from her life. It later brought life when death attacked her son, and it brought restoration of her landed property after the famine (2 Kings 4:8–17, 20–22, 32–36; 2 Kings 8:1–6). Give your time, money, material possessions, and talents for the advancement of God's kingdom. Such giving yields great dividends when mixed with a disposition and language that demonstrates gratitude for the opportunity, not pride and high-mindedness.

4 Serving with Gratitude

The Women (Luke 8:1–3)

Jesus went through towns and villages, preaching the Gospel of the kingdom along with his twelve disciples. Certain women accompanied him and ministered to (served) him with their substance. We are given a sneak peek into the lives and motivation of these women: Mary called Magdalene, out of whom went seven devils; Joanna, the wife of Chuza Herod's steward; Susanna; and many others. These women decided to show gratitude to Jesus for their healings and deliverances by following him and ministering to Him and His disciples. The Amplified Bible says they ministered to and provided for Him out of their property and personal belongings (verse 3 AMP). They served because they were grateful for salvation. In a world in which every form of service rendered demands an exchange of some kind, it has fast become rare to find people serving from a grateful heart. People preach, sing, teach Sunday school, and play musical instruments for pay. Very few are volunteering their services in the house of God. It is entirely scriptural for people to receive financial blessings for services rendered, without necessarily merchandising their gifting and anointing (1 Corinthians 9:13–14). You can, similarly to these women, provide for God's house and work out of your own personal belongings and property. Many who have received healing from HIV/AIDs have decided to furnish the Gospel with the finances that previously went toward their monthly medical expenditures. Their reason was simple—gratitude.

When you serve, you are sowing. Such acts of service will undoubtedly release a harvest back to you, even though your initial reason for serving was not the harvest. The women served and followed Jesus because they were grateful for their healings and deliverances. They followed Him down the pathway to the crucifixion site (Luke 23:27) and witnessed the entire process all the way to the gravesite (Luke 23:48–49, 55–56). Due to their serving with gratitude, they went and prepared spices and ointment for Jesus's body and returned to the tomb very early in the morning (Luke 24:1). They were privileged to receive the announcement of Jesus's resurrection and report to the others because they were service focused even after Jesus's death (Luke 24:2–10; Mark 15:40–42, 47; Mark 16:1–2, 9). These women continued with the rest of the disciples in the upper room (Acts 1:12–14) and experienced the Holy Ghost baptism with the evidence of speaking in other tongues (Acts 2:1–4). They served out of gratitude, and that brought about an unprecedented ripple effect with eternal consequences. They served with no hidden agenda, no ambition to be noticed, and no quest to climb the ladder of recognition or success. They did not even know that their actions would lead them into something greater with lasting impact.

For a graduate who is looking for work right after years of an academic marathon, dropping job applications becomes the order of the day. Losing track of when and where you sent applications is normal. When called for an interview, it is often handled with gratitude, because someone is finally willing to consider hiring you. You are appreciative that someone is willing to give you the chance to prove your worth as a graduate, and even more so because most positions require two years of experience. If this applies to you, do not get into the company and forget to serve honestly and with integrity; show gratitude for the opportunity. Don't get in and start organizing strikes and protests over paper cup supplies!

Grateful people tend to be loyal people. Once a person stops being grateful and starts complaining and criticizing, they cease to be contributors to the team and are toxic and poisonous. Grateful people will give you honest, constructive criticism to enhance growth. An individual who is ungrateful will destructively criticize to tear down. Once a person shifts from being appreciative of a job to complaining about the workplace, their performance level drops, tardiness increases, and they become hard to work with and defiant. Make sure to stay grateful for the people and things you have been blessed with and blessed through, even while transitioning. Gratitude will keep you serving with integrity right to the last minute of your contract or tenure, recognizing that your present location, contacts, and connections were all necessary for your next.

If you are too big to acknowledge the small contributors and contributions to your life, you are too small to receive recognition. We hear countless stories of people whose biological fathers never recognized them from birth and through the growth process. The absence of the father figure creates a vacuum that only intensifies any struggles for the mothers who do their best to assume the position of two-faced parent (the same applies with the absence of a mother figure). Things can get complicated for such families in the advent of the spotlight. For all such absentee parents, there should not be much expectation; coming out of the woodworks and claiming rights and blood connections is a wrong move. If you were too big and too classy to acknowledge such a link to them while they were in need, you are too minute and insignificant for them to give you any recognition whatsoever. If you are one of those parents who tell their children that they are good for nothing, you need to repent and exhibit a change in behavior. Do not come back after they are a success to tell them how you knew all along that they had it in them. You are looking for recognition where you did not sow acknowledgment. Sow determination, tenacity, and confidence in your children so that when they succeed, they will publicly recognize your influence and impact in their lives. Many people want to be a part of what is already successful, to reap the reward without the hard work necessary for success. You are glorified with Jesus only if you suffered with Him (Romans 8:17).

The attitude of gratitude in the women mentioned in Luke 8:1–3 made them serve Jesus with their substance tenaciously, even when it was no longer popular to be associated with Him. They served when most people hailed him for the miracles and healings; they served when He was arrested and tortured; they served all the way to the foot of the cross; they served all the way to the sepulcher and continued serving through His resurrection and ascension. Gratitude will cause you to serve with tenacity and endurance. Never lose the attitude of gratitude. Always find something to be grateful for in every situation. The attitude of gratitude will determine your altitude. The woman who came uninvited into Simon the pharisee's house while Jesus sat at the table brought an alabaster box of ointment. She washed Jesus's feet with her tears, dried them with her hair, kissed them, and anointed them with the ointment. When Simon was disgusted (in his heart) by the entire incident, Jesus used a parable to explain to Simon that this woman's gratitude was the driving force behind her actions (Luke 7:36–47). She was grateful for acceptance and forgiveness, while the pharisee saw her actions as outrageous. In Matthew's account of this occurrence, the disciples described the woman's work as waste; Jesus described it as establishing a memorial (Matthew 26:6–13).

You are distinguished from the crowd when you serve out of gratitude. Some will suggest you are wasting your life or talents, but if you keep the heart thankful and serve with integrity, you will never regret. Those who dare to swim contrary to the direction of the tide always stand out and build a memorial. The rich young ruler who came to Jesus went away sad because Jesus asked him to sell his possessions and give the money to the poor (Mark 10:17–22). He saw that instruction as insane because it would be a waste. On the contrary, Zaccheus was so grateful for acceptance and salvation that he stood up and gave half of all his possessions (Luke 19:1–9). The rich young ruler felt entitled to redemption because he had kept the law from his youth; Zaccheus was grateful to receive the gift of salvation. The latter experienced grace and was grateful, while the former thought he had earned it and deserved it and was arrogant.

Some people start out being grateful and then along the way wallow into faultfinding, murmuring, and complaining because they forget from where they came. Working in a mental health facility, I had the privilege of witnessing homeless people brought off the streets during winter with claims of suicidal ideations. They are grateful for the bed, the roof over their heads, the three square meals a day, the football games they get to watch on television, and so on. As time goes by, some of them begin to complain about the size of their room, not wanting a roommate, requesting extensions on the bedtime schedule because, as adults, they claim they should not be told what to do and when to do it. Soon, they are throwing chairs across the room and demanding to be discharged by their psychiatrist, or they will sign themselves out. They forget that they lived in a cardboard house under a bridge, were uncertain about where their lunch would come from, and did not have the luxury of watching television. May you never forget and become ungrateful!

While on a mission assignment in the Washington, DC, metropolis, my husband and I were elated to discover that there was a place that was serene and saturated by the glory of God. A place we could go and encounter God without cost. This discovery was quite a favor to our lives because, until this time, we missed the glory atmosphere we were accustomed to growing up in the ministry with our pastor. To us, the starvation (as it were) was now over, and we could also grow beyond our previous experiences in the Lord. Furthermore, we found out that the staff (all volunteers) could pick up attendees from the train station, the bus station, or the airport and bring us to the campground at no charge. They would provide two balanced meals a day, serve snacks at night, and a bed at no cost. Moreover, they would pray for you, minister the unadulterated Word of God, and prophesy over you with precision and excellent accuracy. Shockingly, we also heard that they would charge a two-dollar fee for our room key, which was refundable at the time of our departure, should the key be returned to them. We had gone on several retreats before, and we knew the financial sacrifices we had to make for that to happen. Obviously, this was too good to be true. When we arrived at Calvary Pentecostal Campground in Ashland, Virginia (our newly found mystery location), we were so grateful for every opportunity to serve, because we knew how beneficial it was for us to have that experience without having to worry about cost. We volunteered to do whatever the camp needed volunteers to do: vacuuming, cleaning tables after meals, serving in the food line, cleaning restrooms, washing pots, assisting in the prayer lines during services, and so on. It was, and still is an honor and a privilege to serve in whatever way we can, because we are grateful. Only eternity will reveal how much God has accomplished in us, our church members, and others who are connected to us in one way or another through Calvary Pentecostal Tabernacle (CPT) over the years. As pastors, just having a place where we can go and receive personal ministry without fear or favor is priceless. All of these at no charge! We settled with our church family that we will never dare take back the two-dollar refundable deposit because that would be the manifestation of the height of ingratitude and a demonstration of severe ignorance on our part. We serve with gratitude, and we celebrate every opportunity to do so at CPT. Lord, may we never cease to be grateful. God bless CPT!

5 Serving without Comparing or Competing

At the 2013 Fall Women's Convention in CPT, God gave me a vision: I watched as a team of young, vibrant men and women walked into a restaurant for lunch. As they sat at the table, they all placed their orders from the menu. When the food arrived, they all began looking at one another's plate and commenting on the meal options. Some began to salivate over and taste the food choices of the others. Some made casual comments about the food selection of the others—the aroma, the taste, the layout and presentation, the quantity. Some liked what others had ordered and commented as such but still preferred what they had ordered for themselves. Others liked what someone else had ordered to the point that they began to regret having ordered something different. They remained in disappointment and misery and failed to enjoy the food that they initially requested with excitement. Disappointment and grief came in as they compared their food with that of others and dwelled on the difference.

When I began to pray in tongues, searching for an understanding of the vision, God said many in the body of Christ do not serve Him in the capacity of their assignment because they are busy comparing themselves with others, trying to be like others, and wanting to do like others. When you become competitive, you can become ungrateful. You tend to focus on what someone else has and become blind to what you have received. Some people are afraid to venture into their God-given assignment because they compare themselves with those in the field and feel inadequate.

You give yourself reasons why you do not think success is possible because you compare yourself with other successful people and quickly conclude that they are better than you. You tell God to assign someone more intelligent, more eloquent, wiser, and stronger than you, and yes, one with more educational qualifications. God saw all of those people but decided that you were the one for the job.

The first time I ever stepped foot in a library was a defining day in my life, as I would later notice. I saw a huge placard on one of the walls with a poem titled "Desiderata." I read the whole thing several times, as I was intrigued by the wisdom of whoever the author was. They spoke directly to me, with vivid instructions on how I ought to live my life. One of the truths that jumped off that wall directly into my heart was this: if you compare yourself with others, you may become vain and bitter, for always there will be greater and lesser persons than yourself. At that young age, I remember thinking, *Hmmm! Be yourself. It's cheaper*, as I read through some of the words too bogus for my young brain to comprehend. I ran into the library just to make sure that I read "Desiderata" daily, until this genius idea hit me: *Why don't I just sit down and write it out and take it with me? That way I can read it whenever I want, rather than let library hours limit me.* This was back in the day when computers and printers were unheard of in the school libraries, let alone internet. No! Not in my part of the world. I can still see my young self, sitting in that library away from the window to focus, painstakingly writing out the entire poem. I read it daily and sometimes more than once a day for many years until I could recite the whole thing.

Be you! Allow yourself the liberty to be you, with room for growth in your uniqueness. Fear of not being as successful as somebody else should not stop you from stepping out. No one can beat you at your best. If your assignment is establishing educational institutions, do not try to do television just because all seemingly successful preachers are on TV. Stay in your lane and obey God. Your acceptable act of worship is in your obedience. In John 21:14–22, Jesus told Peter to mind his business and stop comparing himself with John but rather focus on following Him. No one has made you a judge over another man's servant (Romans 14:4). Focus on your personal assignment and follow Jesus. Whatever God chooses to do with any of His children is none of your business. You do not have the permission to sin because another child of God sinned and seemingly got away with it. The Word of God is the yardstick, not humans. Fix your eyes on Jesus and keep walking. Serve without competing or comparing.

Ruth and Orpah were both daughters-in-law to Naomi, and they had lost their husbands. After losing her husband and both her sons, Naomi decided to leave the land of Moab and return to her own country of Bethlehem-Judah. Ruth and Orpah went with their mother-in-law. After much persuasion from Naomi, Orpah accepted going back to her people, but Ruth refused to let Naomi go (Ruth 1:6–14). Ruth stood her ground on her decision to follow Naomi, even when Naomi tried to convince her by comparing her to Orpah. She told her that Orpah had returned to her people, and it would be wise if she did the same (Ruth 1:15). Ruth refused to fall under the power of competition and comparison. She was convicted about her stand, and it was not going to be affected by Orpah's decision. When Naomi saw that Ruth was steadfast and would not budge, she stopped pushing (Ruth 1:17–18). Ruth focused on her convictions about serving her mother-in-law, with whom she had already spent ten years of her life. There was no clear future in this decision because Naomi had no other son for her to marry. Naomi was uncertain about what she was returning to after being away for so long, but her uncertainties did not derail Ruth in any way. She focused on her assignment of serving Naomi, though it seemed like a waste of her life and a bad business decision. There was a certainty in her spirit that kept her tenacious in her service. She did not realize that she stuck out like a sore thumb in Bethlehem-Judah, due to her excellence in service to her dead husband's mother. Boaz noticed her, began asking questions, and was furnished with answers that only impressed him the more (Ruth 2:11–12).

When your focus is service unto the Lord, without competitive ambition to get ahead or outdo anyone else, you become reputable and notable. They saw her as an epitome of selflessness and servanthood because serving Naomi was a dead-end job with no paycheck and no prospects. The town talked about Ruth the Moabitess who followed her mother-in-law into a foreign land, served her to provide for her well-being, without expecting a reward, and paid no attention to herself but only to her assignment. Boaz eventually married her, and she became the great-grandmother of David (Ruth 4:17). The elders at the gate released blessings on this marriage and the fruit of it (Ruth 4:11–15). Boaz met Ruth at a place of service, not because she was looking for a husband. In the Christian circles, we constantly hear unwed sisters talking about waiting for their Boaz. It has become such a cliché because very few are doing what Ruth did. No one is saying that you have to quit your job and go live with your late husband's mother and wait on her hand and foot—unless God tells you expressly, of course. Are you serving where you are, while expecting your Boaz? How is your service unto the Lord?

In scripture, most outstanding women encountered their future husbands while they were in a place of duty, serving faithfully. Abraham's servant met Rebekah at the well, on his way to find the wife for his master's son, Isaac (Genesis 24:42–46). Drawing water and watering cattle is hard work. Jacob met Rachel at the well, where she brought her father's cattle to water them because she kept the flock (Genesis 30:6–9). King David met Abigail at a place of service in intercession for her family (1 Samuel 25:18–23). Moses met Zipporah, along with her six sisters, at a well (Exodus 2:15–21). My husband and I met while I was preaching the Gospel through door-to-door evangelism.

Hallelujah! These women did not set out looking for mates. They were serving, and their spouses met them at a place of service. Take your position on duty and keep doing the work of the ministry. There is no telling who might find you, and that will bring glory to God.

This is not limited to marriage. I am in no way suggesting that your only motivation for serving should be to get married. A place of service will position you to meet with the greatness that will change your life forever. If you asked the Samaritan woman who met Jesus at the well, she would tell you she was not in search of another man. She had already had five husbands and was currently living with a man to whom she had no marriage ties. She knew how to get them, so she had no struggles in that department. But her life was empty, and she was thirsty for something more. Her encounter with greatness that day at that well changed her entire life and turned her into a renowned evangelist in less than twenty-four hours (John 4:39). Rahab's service of hospitality toward the spies completely changed the predicted fatal outcome for her family (Joshua 2:1, 18–21; 6:22–25). The widow of Zarephath knew that fateful day was her last on earth, when she met with the prophet Elijah as she gathered sticks for her son's last meal. That encounter marked the end of the famine in her house, even though the rest of the land was still in starvation, and brought her son back to life after he died (1 Kings 17:8–24). All these blessings came to her because she lodged the man of God in her home. Diligence in service will cause you to stand before kings and not mean men (Proverbs 22:29).

You could be in the wrong profession, unpleasant job, or even uninspiring assignment and be drowned by a sense of unfulfillment and feelings of meanness, only because your friends are seemingly making a lot of money doing that. You could be in the wrong assignment in ministry because you are competing with others for prominence. You may be married to the wrong spouse because all your peers were getting married before you, and you felt the need to prove a point. If you place money above assignment or calling, you may pursue the wrong career that God never intended for you. This explains why many people are miserable at their jobs, demonstrating underrated customer service skills, with no compassion toward the people they are supposedly serving. Every career is an opportunity to serve. Are you serving your assigned crowd? Are you reaching your target audience? Do you even know that you have a designated crowd or target audience? If God put a passion in you for young people, to encourage and help them become great in life, why are you working in a nursing home or car sales shop or even an assisted-living facility with seniors? Why are you not working at a youth empowerment center as a life coach? Is it because someone convinced you that there is better pay or job security with health caregivers? Are you pastoring a church because you responded to a pastor-wanted ad with appealing incentives in the employment package? Or is it because God has called you as a pastor? Are you a medical doctor because everyone in your family is expected to be a lawyer, a doctor, or an engineer to be considered successful?

Your lack of fulfillment may be a result of that. You are busy taking care of another person's vineyard while yours is in ruins.

Paul declared that as a wise master builder, he laid the foundation according to the grace given him (1 Corinthians 3:10). He goes on to warn that everyone must take heed how they build upon that foundation. You must build according to the grace given you. Serving with competition and comparison will cause you to walk in a graceless zone. In Romans 12:3–8, the apostle Paul admonishes the believer to stay away from competition, knowing that each person is called unto a particular task with the divine enablement (grace) to function therein. You must wait on your ministering (Romans 12:7). We are one body with different body parts having different functions. You must operate according to the grace given, according to the proportion of faith (Romans 12:5–6). No comparison! No competition! You are unique! Paul rebuked the Corinthian church, calling them carnal babies because they were comparing him with Apollos, thereby introducing strife and division (1 Corinthians 3:1–8). Comparison and competition are signs of carnality and childishness. Grow up! We shall all receive rewards according to our work and based on our personal walk and assignment. One person's task is to plant, while the other's is to water what has been planted. God, the Giver of increase, gets the glory and the credit. No mature servant seeks the credit. They give God credit and look forward to their reward for faithful service (Matthew 25:23). Jesus said the following in Luke 17:10 Amplified Bible (AMP):

So you too, when you have done everything that was assigned and commanded you, say, "We are unworthy servants [undeserving of praise or a reward, for we have not gone beyond our obligation]; we have merely done what we ought to do."

If you leave your intercessory assignment and decide to pastor a church, you are in a graceless zone, even though you can preach. John made a significant statement of truth in John 3:27: a man can receive nothing except it be given him from heaven. He said this in response to an attack by the spirit of competition. The disciples of John were trying to tell him that the person he baptized was now baptizing other people. In other words, the person you ushered into ministry and to whom you gave all those connections is now starting a church one block away from your church. The friend you helped to get employment at your place of work is now approved for the managerial position you wanted. What do you do? When you settle within you that everything you have and want should come from God, competition dies from your life. You will be free from the torments of insecurity and fear. No one can take your place if you just stay in your lane and do what God has called you to do. Insecure people are individuals who do not know their assignment.

John reminded his disciples how he had told them that he was merely the voice in the wilderness, not the Messiah. He told them that he must now decrease for Jesus to increase

(John 3:22–31; John 1:19–27). Knowledge of your assignment will kill competition and insecurity. Staying in the place of your assignment ensures that you are not threatened by the success and achievements of others but rather are in celebration of them. The apostles showed great maturity by giving Paul the right hand of fellowship, as they recognized the call of God on his life to the Gentiles (Galatians 2:8–9). If you feel threatened by the success of others, go to God in prayer for a reaffirmation of who you are in Him. Isn't it amazing to see a Shell gas station next to Exxon and they both wear their names proudly and are both thriving in business?

The problem is neither the arrogant nor the obnoxious way in which that person behaves; the real problem is your lack of self-identity. Who are you? Moment of truth! Do you often fight to prove a point? Do you always make statements to establish the obvious about your status and position? Do you arrogantly mention your achievements and successes when you speak? Do you fight to prove what is obvious? Are you physically or verbally abusive to your wife to show her that you are the man of the house? Have you raised your voice uncharacteristically to show an employee that you are the boss? All these are red flags of poor self-worth and lack of identity.

Satan asked Jesus to prove the obvious, but Jesus did not fall for that temptation: if you are the Son of God (Matthew 4:3, 6). The temptation was never about Jesus eating bread. Neither was it about angels' ability to protect His feet but rather about His identity as the Son of God. Derailment can happen to you regarding your assignment, if you lose sight of your purpose. Aggressively come against things that sabotage your identity in Christ because the purpose of that attack is to make you an unprofitable servant. After the first two temptations that focused on attacking His identity, the third one targeted His assignment. Satan offered to give Jesus the world if He would only bow down and worship him (Matthew 4:8–9). It presented an easier route than crucifixion to reclaim the world, didn't it? How often have you changed God's instructions because another option was introduced to you?

All roads do not lead to Rome, contrary to popular opinion. You must carry out your assignment following the command you received. Jesus did not say, "Yeah, this might work; moreover, I'll still reclaim the world and not even have to die for it. I just bow down once, and that's it. Easy enough." Stop compromising the instructions of God for less combative routes and alternatives. Stick to God's plan and build according to the pattern and blueprint given you by God. If God says you should win souls one at a time at your workplace, don't say you would rather organize an outdoor open-air crusade. That is somebody else's assignment. We all are laborers with God, accomplishing the same goal of advancing the kingdom, using different God-given tools and strategies. When one of his disciples told him that he stopped someone from casting out devils because he was not part of their fold, Jesus responded by saying (among other things) that those who were not against them were for them (Mark 9:36–40). Stop fighting fellow ministers and get back to kingdom business. The television network is someone's assigned tool to reach the lost who would not otherwise come to the local church. The local church is strategically positioned to get God's people nurtured, fed, and equipped for the work of the kingdom. We need one another. Let us serve our Father alongside one another, not against one another.

Never measure your success by comparing with others. To rightly measure success, use the instruction from the Master who called you. Success is therefore an obedience test.

> For we dare not make ourselves of the number, or compare ourselves with some that commend themselves: but they measuring themselves by themselves, and comparing themselves among themselves, are not wise. But we will not boast of things without our measure, but according to the measure of the rule which God had distributed to us, a measure to reach even unto you. For we stretch not ourselves beyond our measure, as though we reached not unto you: for we are come as far as to you also in preaching the gospel of Christ: Not boasting of things without our measure, that is, of other men's labours; but having hope, when your faith is increased, that we shall be enlarged by you according to our rule abundantly, to preach the gospel in the regions beyond you, and not to boast in another man's line of things made

ready to our hand. But he that glorieth, let him glory in the Lord. For not he that commendeth himself is approved, but whom the Lord commendeth. (2 Corinthians 10:12–18)

Serve right—according to divine assignment and enablement. Refuse graceless zones.

6 Serving in Transparency— No Hidden Agenda

When you apply for a job, most often your résumé will read something like this: "young, enthusiastic person looking for a challenging opportunity with room for growth." It indicates, in an honest and upfront way, your aspirations for growth on the corporate ladder. It reveals that you are ambitious and looking forward to growing within that company as you prove your worth with every service opportunity. This understanding is beautiful and noble. Ambition in itself is not evil, and there is nothing wrong with being increase minded. It becomes dangerous when your motives are shady and you will stop at nothing, even if it means deliberately stepping on toes and dragging others down. It poses a real problem if, after being employed for janitorial duties at a hospital, you have ambitions of becoming the director of nursing, with no health care knowledge or skill and no intention of acquiring the much-needed knowledge.

Many have sought to serve in positions and roles because they saw flamboyance and fame. If this describes you, you can repent and get realigned. Jesus spoke against the attitude of the pharisees, who prayed standing on street corners "to be seen by men." He was not speaking against praying in a public gathering, as some have tried to suggest, but against why they did it. He said they already had their reward (Matthew 6:1–6). Simply put, if you do any service with a hidden agenda of wanting to be seen, you might as well enjoy the fame while it lasts, because that is all the reward you will ever get for that service.

Service is not intended for a spotlight, stardom, and fame. The kingdom's purpose is not to create celebrities out of us. Ministry means service. It is not for men and women to build empires for themselves. Your obedience to God will bring you fame and greatness, but fame is not the goal. God promises to increase you and make your name great. It is for Him to do that, to make you a shining example of what happens to the person who wholeheartedly serves Him. The fame of Jesus was noised abroad as he went about doing what he saw his Father do, but he was not doing so in order to be famous (Luke 5:14–15). No one serves a great God and remains small! Notwithstanding, never serve with the motive of searching for fame. God alone deserves the glory and credit. Serve to make Him famous!

A mother in the faith shared with me an illustration that God gave her regarding this. God said she was His representative; therefore, everything meant for God would be done to her: "A room is prepared for Him, but you get to sleep in it. The financial gift is an offering to Him, but you have the privilege of collecting. The table is prepared for Him, but you get to eat on His behalf. The praises, as well as the insults, were equally meant for Him, but you get the distinct pleasure of receiving them for Him. Now, you have to make sure that you give God all that you receive in His place—the praises and the insults, the credit, and the blame. Do not own any." When she was done talking, I remember sitting still for a moment, not sure what sparked the story but recognizing a God moment. I quickly scanned my life, making sure I have given Him everything I have ever received on His behalf. I also repented for every instance in which I had owned anything meant for Him. It was a holy moment, which still sends shivers down my spine as I recount it. I will never forget such moments in the presence of greatness, when nuggets dropped into my spirit through those ancient wells (my terminology to describe mothers and fathers in the faith). This was priceless to me, and it has carried me through some troubled waters. That profound truth came from Pastor Jane Lowder, director of Calvary Pentecostal Tabernacle in Ashland, Virginia. Thank you, Pastor Jane!

When Joseph served God in prison by interpreting the butler's dream, he tried to use that service as a ladder to climb out of jail. He told the butler to put in a good word for him to Pharaoh (Genesis 40:14–15), but the butler forgot all about him when he got out (Genesis 40:23). Joseph, a long while later (two years), was called to interpret Pharaoh's dream. This time around, he gave the interpretation without any hidden agenda (Genesis 41:1, 33). Then God touched Pharaoh, and he appointed Joseph as the executor of God's counsel and direction (Genesis 41:38–42). Learn to serve God, obeying His leadings without self-promoting and self-advertising. Do you use the prophetic gift to make yourself famous? Do you use ministry doors to further your personal interests, or do you use these doors to reach and serve more people for His glory? Let God elevate you, and stop trying so hard to announce yourself.

Ruth served her mother-in-law in total transparency. Her heart was right, and she had no hidden motives. All she wanted to do was ensure the well-being of her widowed, old, and childless in-law. She went to the fields to glean barley behind the reapers, working from morning until night. She was not found making idle conversation by the water cooler in the break room. She had an impeccable work ethic. And she did not do this to be noticed but out of the integrity of her heart. She was not on anyone's clock because she was not an employee, yet she had a unique work ethic that made her noticeable. When Boaz asked about her, the head of the reapers gave an impressive résumé regarding her work ethic (Ruth 2:5–7).

Do you have transparency in your activities? How would you describe your work ethic? Do you have meaningless conversations on company time? Do you use company time to surf the internet about personal matters without permission? Do you have someone else punch in for you at work before you get there? Are you always late? Is your break time always thirty to forty-five minutes longer than the time allocated by the company? Do you secretly collect company supplies for your personal use later (stealing)? Do you actually earn what you make at your job, or receive payment for work you do not do? Do you get any real work done when your supervisor is not around? Nature has a way of rewarding integrity and hard work because creation measures every person's work and releases their reward.

In the account mentioning the ascension of Ruth to a place of recognition, she asked Boaz why he was good to her. He responded by saying, "I have been made fully aware of all you have done for your mother-in-law since the death of your husband" (Ruth 2:10–11). Boaz goes on to declare blessings and recompense over her from the Lord (i.e., heavenly reward for work done) (Ruth 2:12). Ruth's private commitment to Naomi became common knowledge. Integrity is who you are and what you do when no one is watching. Ruth's husband and father-in-law had died, and there was nobody in Naomi's life that Ruth could have been trying to impress. Naomi painted a vivid picture of the gloomy situation to her in an attempt to deter her from wasting the rest of her life (Ruth 1:11–13). She knew what she was committed to doing, and she served with total transparency. All Ruth ever wanted was to ensure the well-being of Naomi. God's recompense for her integrity and transparent service was far more beneficial than she could ever dream. She married one of the wealthiest men in the land and became the co-owner of the fields from which she gleaned.

> Slaves, be obedient to those who are your earthly masters, with respect for authority, and with a sincere heart [seeking to please them], as [service] to Christ—not in the way of eye-service [working only when someone is watching you and only] to please men, but as

slaves of Christ, doing the will of God from your heart. (Ephesians 6:5–6 AMP)

The thief [who has become a believer] must no longer steal, but instead he must work hard [making an honest living], producing that which is good with his own hands, so that he will have something to share with those in need. (Ephesians 4:28 AMP)

And in all things show yourself to be an example of good works, with purity in doctrine [having the strictest regard for integrity and truth], dignified. (Titus 2:7 AMP)

[Tell] bond servants to be submissive to their masters, to be pleasing and give satisfaction in every way. [Warn them] not to talk back or contradict, Nor to steal by taking things of small value, but to prove themselves truly loyal and entirely reliable and faithful throughout, so that in everything they may be an ornament and do credit to the teaching [which is] from and about God our Savior. (Titus 2:9–10 AMPC)

Never speak negatively about an institution or company to others, whether as a former or current employee. If you have concerns, voice them using the appropriate channel provided by that corporation. You have the right to quit if you do not agree with their methods or standards of operation, but you are not allowed to speak of them in a derogatory manner. Differences in mode of operation, standards, and ethical or economic issues do not qualify that company or institution as an enemy to you. Watch your motive. Serve in transparency, as unto the Lord, not unto humans. Do not poison the minds of the people in the company before leaving. Your motive is devilish and diabolical if you conspire to poison the minds of church members because you do not agree with the leadership. You just made yourself an agent of darkness to destroy God's work, no matter the validity of your concern.

Beware of the attitude of Absalom. He was known to stand in the courts and talk with those who came from meetings with the king. In doing so, he gave his two cents' contribution in royal counsel, undermining the king and suggesting that he would have provided a better alternative. His motive was to gain recognition. It is a demonic disposition that causes you to serve with a hidden agenda to overthrow the existing authority and take over. It is the attempt of usurping authority by primarily infiltrating an institution in the guise of being an integral part of that organization. Similar behavior is exhibited by someone who is serving in the choir of the church, while privately poisoning the minds of the other singers and musicians against the choir leader, with the intention of becoming the choir leader or for other power hungry gains. You are an Absalom, and you must repent! You say, "If I were the leader, we would have more lead singers, fewer rehearsals, and more freedom to wear whatever we want. I don't understand what the leader is thinking." You pretend to be genuinely concerned about the productivity of your department, and you bypass your immediate supervisor to go and present some new ideas to your supervisor's boss.

After bowing before his father, the king, Absalom would stand at the king's gate and speak to the people as they came in to see the king for their disputes to be settled. He would hear the king's verdict from them and then tell them that if he were the king, he would have done it differently (2 Samuel 14:33; 15:2–13). He acted as though he was submitted to the king, while he stole the hearts of the people from King David. What a manifestation of false allegiance and hypocrisy!

Are you serving in transparency or conspiracy? Are you acting humble and submissive to win the trust of leadership while organizing a revolution behind the leader's back? Are you working your way into the inner circle of an organization or company using false allegiance, while masterminding a plan to take over the position of influence and authority? If yes, you have the tendencies of Absalom, and you will end up like him if you do not repent. "God shall not be mocked," scripture says. If you conspired to start a church with half the membership of your former church, behind the pastor's back, you will not go far in life. You cannot build anything with lasting value by tearing down someone else's building. You cannot build a sustainable business, company, church, or relationship with bricks stolen from another. It will crumble with time, unless you repent. If your current spouse is a product of an adulterous affair, you will lose that wife or husband to adultery if you do not repent. If you started a church with members of another congregation or ministry, due to scheming tricks, you will lose them all to the next crafty pastor like yourself.

There is no justification for conspiracy. It is a bad seed that will yield a massive harvest of its kind. Another outwitted Ahithophel, who betrayed King David to gain recognition in Absalom's reign, resulting in him hanging himself (2 Samuel 17:14, 23). Absalom's death was nothing short of creation payback. On the day of his death, trees killed more people than the sword. He got caught in an oak tree, after which Joab drove three darts through his heart. As if that was not enough, ten young men who were armor bearers to Joab smote him and slew him (2 Samuel 18:8–10, 14–15).

The life of Samuel is an example of transparent service. His mother, Hannah, brought him to the temple as a fulfillment of a vow she made to the Lord. Samuel grew and ministered to the Lord, being a child, and had favor with the Lord and men (1 Samuel 2:18, 26). The sons of Eli the priest, on the other hand, were not living right before the Lord. God was displeased with Eli for not correcting his children (1 Samuel 2:27–36; 3:11–14).

By the way, God has put you in charge of your kids to train them in the ways of the Lord and to discipline them when they misbehave. Arise and handle your business as a parent. Be your child's parent, not their buddy at the expense of proper parenting. Samuel served God under the old priest Eli, whose eyes had gone dim, and he remained respectful of him. When God told Samuel what He planned to do to Eli and his sons, Samuel did not jubilate and say, "Here is my opportunity to become the one in charge." He was afraid for Eli and feared to tell him the vision. When Eli persuaded him, he was honest and transparent, hiding nothing (1 Samuel 3:18 AMP). Despite his knowledge of the priest's flaws, Samuel served with transparent accountability. The Bible records that all Israel knew that Samuel was established to be a prophet of the Lord (1 Samuel 3:19–20). God honored Samuel's service to Eli and did not let any of his words fall to the ground. Samuel did not go telling everybody about his vision and how God revealed to him that Eli was evil.

Many people celebrate when others fail or when others do not succeed as well as they have. They envy those who progress and secretly wish they would fall. This explains why they get on their phones and announce the mistakes and mishaps to as many people as will listen. When you have to bring down someone else to feel good about yourself, you need to take your heart to the altar of God. We must master discretion and transparency. Some people gossip and call it transparency. Then they get sneaky and call it discretion. Samuel was transparent with Eli in telling him all that God said; he was discrete with the information and therefore did not tell anyone else. Very often at the workplace, there is so much character assassination going on, just as in the churches and in political circles, all in the guise of being transparent or concerned. Check your motives, and you will know exactly why you do what you do. If you are trying to hinder another person's progress by distorting the way others see them, you are manipulative. God could trust Samuel with the greater responsibility of ruling the people of Israel because he had proven himself in the smaller matters of discretion, transparency, and accountability. People around you with poor accountability skills should raise a red flag for any leader, because it signals a hidden agenda. They exercise authority on your behalf without your permission and fail to report their activities to you. Have you had an employee speak on your behalf, close a deal in your place, or settle an issue in your name but fail to tell you what they did? Watch out! None of that is random. They may be establishing their brand with your clients, using your resources, hiding in plain sight. Do you have church leaders who counsel the members in your place but fail to report to you? Do you get to find out when things go wrong that there were meetings where people acted in your name, when you never assigned them to do so? Watch out!

Hebrews 12:15 (AMPC) says, "Exercise foresight and be on the watch to look [after one another], to see that no one falls back from and fails to secure God's grace (His unmerited favor and spiritual blessing), in order that no root of resentment (rancor, bitterness, or hatred) shoots forth and causes trouble and bitter torment, and the many become contaminated and defiled by it." If you are one of those representing a different course, other than that of the company or institution you claim to be working for, you are operating in witchcraft (1 Samuel 15:23). Do not use another person's vision as a platform for yours; it creates division. Stop misrepresenting the company that pays you to represent it. If you no longer agree with their cause or course, respectfully turn in your resignation. Do not step out in their name, using their resources to push your private and personal agenda. That is demonic, no matter how noble and righteous you may sound.

Gehazi ended up with leprosy because he acted in Elisha's name, misrepresenting the man of God for his personal gain. The prophet Elisha had already refused the gifts offered by Naaman, the leprous Syrian commander, who got healed. Gehazi, his servant, did not approve of his master's decision regarding the donations. He therefore followed Naaman and lied to him, saying that Elisha had changed his mind, and sent him to collect the gifts (2 Kings 5:15–22). When Gehazi returned from his secretive, greedy adventure, he could not be accountable to his master. He was dishonest with Elisha when the prophet asked him where he had been (2 Kings 5:24–25). Never ignore the warning signs of falsehood and secrecy manifested by people in your circle. If you do, their betrayal will take you unawares and wallop you with far-reaching consequences. When they begin to lie to you or conveniently forget to report vital information, it is time to call out these intentional omissions and call them to order. They do not deserve the level of access and influence you have given them. You may have to withdraw some of the access and influence until you are sure about where their loyalties lie.

Ananias and Sapphira loved to belong but were unwilling to serve in transparency. We are told that they sold their land and brought part of the money to the apostles but were dishonest, saying that they brought all of it. The problem was not that they brought part; it was theirs, same as the land, and they had the right to do as they wanted. The problem was in the fact that they were dishonest to the apostles about it. Apostle Peter said they lied to the Holy Ghost (Acts 5:3–4). Be transparent in your service to the Lord, regarding your tithes and offerings. This is about you and God, not the pastor of the church. Bring your first tenth to God, not any tenth. It is about honor, not about money. "The way you do anything is the way you do everything," I heard someone say in a business training session I attended. If we do not give defective gifts to those we honor, why give it to God? (Malachi 1:5–8). When you provide an offering with the motive of wanting to be hailed and praised, you will have no reward from God. You have a hidden agenda, and God will not honor your gift (Matthew 6:1–4). Your giving is not a money test or possession test; it is a heart test. Does God truly have your heart? If He does, He will have your pocketbook too (Matthew 6:20–21). Be a good and profitable steward, ready to release to the Master and Owner whatever He demands from you. God is the one who gives you the power to make wealth, for the purpose of advancing the kingdom (Deuteronomy 8:18). Release with joy and honor God with your substance—actually His in your care.

You! Yes, you! If you have been doing your best to serve in transparency but happen to have a boss or leader who uses your transparency to hurt you, do not be alarmed. You are not alone. And yes, there is such a thing as a leader threatened by the abilities of the one they are leading. God protects His own when you choose to do right (1 Peter 3:13). Trust God for the appropriate wisdom in your dealings with this authority, without you becoming the leader you are criticizing. David served under King Saul, who was insecure and threatened by the perceived future of David. Saul would throw spears at David but missed every single time because of God's protection. And Saul feared David even more (1 Samuel 18:11–15). Never once did David throw a spear back at Saul. Learn from David, who genuinely served Saul even after he had been anointed by Samuel to take Saul's place. He respected and honored Saul as the Lord's anointed, refusing to kill him when the opportunity presented itself (1 Samuel 26:8–11). David painstakingly tried to reason with King Saul, to convince him of his loyalty and transparency in his dealings with Saul (1 Samuel 26:17–27). God kept David covered until he transitioned to the throne without destroying his personal testimony by usurping authority. Trust God and do the right thing. God who keeps Israel neither slumbers nor sleeps! No weapon formed against you will prosper. God will protect you and deliver you from evil. David learned from Saul what not to do when he became king. Learn what this situation is teaching you and do not waste your trial. "If a man's ways please the Lord, he will cause his enemies to be at peace with him" (Proverbs 16:7). Proverbs 21:1 says the king's heart is in the Lord's hand. Pray in the Spirit and listen to the Spirit's leading. Walk in love and refuse the countless opportunities presented to you for revenge or rebellion. Vengeance belongs to the Lord, not you (Romans 12:17–21). If you do not know Jesus as your personal Lord and Savior, this is the perfect moment to receive Him—because you *need* Him. Ask Him to take over your life and help you step by step. If you did, then know He did. You need God on your side to escape and survive an all-out war from a leader who is out to annihilate you and yours. Study the transition of Jacob from Laban's authority in Genesis 31; refuse to make fear-driven decisions (Genesis 31:31); trust that the God who said it was time to transition is able to touch the heart of your leader to release you. May you experience a peaceful transition in Jesus's name! Rejoice, knowing it will all work out for your good. All is well!

7 Serving with Initiative

There are many companies in the world. Each of these companies differs from the other in structure and function. Organizations tend to teach their employees the core culture that drives the company's success. New recruits must go through a period of orientation when hired into a new job or position. The purpose of the orientation is to familiarize you with the demands of your job description. Your employer does not assume that you know and understand all the protocols and therefore assigns someone to work with you for a given period, to facilitate your assignment. After the orientation phase, you are expected to function every day at work, carrying out the responsibilities of your job description without a reminder from your immediate supervisor. If you hired a personal secretary and have to remind them to answer the phone each time it rings, something is seriously wrong. In the same vein, God's Word clearly stipulates our job description as disciples of Jesus Christ, yet so many children of God seem idle because they do not have a title.

You do not need a title to lay hands on the sick, cast out devils, speak with new tongues, or preach the Gospel to every creature. These are some of the signs that follow the believer (Mark 16:15–18). A general knowledge of what is expected of you by your King Jesus should enable you to serve Him with initiative, regardless of the presence of a title or the absence thereof. Those who get hung up on titles have inferiority complex issues that need resolving. If you are waiting to be appointed deacon before you see the need to visit a sick brother, something is seriously off.

There is an end-time revival coming, and it will break forth through the nameless and faceless people in the ministry of helps who position themselves to be used by God for whatever He wants to be done. People will be healed from incurable diseases as the praise and worship team engages God in genuine worship; people will be slain in the restrooms because the janitors prayed in tongues as they cleaned the toilets the day before. Sinners will cry out for Jesus before the start of service as they listen to the instrumentals playing through the sound system because the media team was soaked in prayer as they got the microphones ready for service. Someone will get healed by shaking the hand of an usher at the entrance as they are directed to a seat. That is the revival of positioning! It shall not be a one-man show, but disciples of Jesus all over the world will take their rightful place, strategically positioned for the end-time harvest, and they will move in the Spirit because they have a relationship with Jesus. This is a movement, and it is upon us *now*. Get positioned!

In Acts 9:36–42, we are introduced to Tabitha (Dorcas), a disciple of Jesus Christ. She served by taking the initiative in the house of God. She looked around and saw a need, which apparently coincided with a skill set that she had. As a dressmaker, she saw that some believers could use some new clothes, or at least some decent ones. So she went to work. She took the initiative to serve God by providing clothes for His people. When she died, the believers refused to bury her but rather sent for Peter to come and raise her back to life. The widows wept and displayed the coats and garments she had made for them. Her service toward them made her indispensable, and they released their faith for her to be raised from death. "God is not unrighteous to forget your work and labor of love, which you have shown toward His name, in that you have ministered to the saints, and do minister" (Hebrews 6:10). When you see a need, step up, take the initiative, and do for God without looking for a camera crew to broadcast your actions. Galatians 6:10 says, "As we have therefore opportunity let us do good unto all men, especially unto them who are of the household of faith." Dorcas served with initiative, without a title, and her voice was heard louder in death because her service lived. Your voice as a servant speaks life!

Are you serving while mindful of taking the initiative? Do you pick up the trash in the hallway as you walk through or skip over it because you are not part of housekeeping department? Do you walk away from the sink full of dirty dishes because you are not part of the kitchen staff? Do you hold the elevator door for the stranger who is clearly struggling to get in? Do you lend a helping hand to the single mother who might be struggling with two grocery bags, a toddler, and an infant as she makes her way to her car after a long day's work? Do you return your shopping cart in the designated area or do you abandon it in the middle of the parking lot because "someone gets paid to do that"? Do you put in more paper in the copier after using the last one? How about a fresh roll of toilet paper? Would you, as a health care provider, give a patient a fresh cup of ice water, even if that patient was not part of your room assignment for the day? Are you one of those who will walk away saying, "That's not my patient"? Scripture admonishes us to pursue the practice of hospitality (Romans 12:13 AMP).

> Do not neglect to extend hospitality to strangers [especially among the family of believers— being friendly, cordial, and gracious, sharing the comforts of your home and doing your part generously], for by this some have entertained angels without knowing it. (Hebrews 13:2 AMP)

In Genesis 24, we are told of a classic example of an exceptional young woman who served with initiative and became the wife of Isaac. Her name is Rebekah. When Eliezer (Abraham's servant) set out in search of a wife for Isaac (his master's son and heir), he asked the Lord of his master to direct him to the woman ordained for Isaac. He requested that it would be the woman who, when he asked for some water, would take the initiative to offer water to all of his camels too (verses 12–14). Eliezer did not have two camels; he had ten! We are told that camels can go for up to six months without drinking any water, which made them an ideal mode of transportation in the desert for centuries. A very thirsty camel, such as the one just off a long, hot caravan like Eliezer's, can gulp thirty-five gallons of water in six minutes (onekindplanet.org; amazing facts about the camel). Eliezer had ten camels (verse 10). It has to be a whole day's work to draw water from the well with a pitcher, enough to satisfy ten camels from a far country. Rebekah not only gave Eliezer water to drink, but she also took the initiative (knowing the cost and sacrifice) to draw water for all of his camels. Watch her language and disposition of service:

> And she said, Drink, my lord: and she hasted, and let down her pitcher upon her hand, and gave him drink.

> And when she had done giving him drink, she said, I will draw water for thy camels also, until they have done drinking.

> And she hasted, and emptied her pitcher into the trough, and ran again unto the well to draw water, and drew for all his camels. (Genesis 24:18–20 KJV)

The speed and precision with which this happened caused Eliezer to stand and gaze at her in silence, waiting to know if the Lord had made his trip prosperous (Genesis 24:21 AMP). Have you ever had God answer a prayer request of yours while you are still praying? Eliezer was in amazement because God answered before he was done praying (verse 15).

Eliezer knew instantly that Rebekah was wife material. He put gold earrings and bracelets on her, and she became Isaac's wife. Her ability to serve with initiative, coupled with her language and disposition of service, made her outstanding. Are you wife material? Are you waiting for a spouse, yet your nature does not reflect service? Marriage is ministry (service), and if you jump into marriage without developing these elements of service in your life, you may make a mess of your union. If you are already married and struggling with this, you can learn and grow. This applies to both men and women. It is such a misconception in certain circles that only the woman is to prepare for marriage. We are supposed to serve each other within the matrimonial covenant if we are to have successful marriages worth emulating. The church, the bride of Christ, must be wife material.

How far are you willing to go to serve? Can you give someone a ride to a destination that is not in the direction you were headed? Jesus put it this way: "And whosoever shall compel thee to go a mile, go with him twain" (Matthew 5:41). Can you take the initiative of paying the whole bill when you go out to eat with friends? When a friend gives you a ride, do you fill up the gas tank? Do you step up and engage the first-time church visitor who seems to be standing in a corner all alone? Instead of looking at a situation and saying, "Why don't they do …? Why don't they have …?" you can take the initiative to serve in that area where you see the vacancy or discrepancy, of course with consent from authority where needed. Everything must be done decently and in order.

There is plenty to do in service to God, both in His church and in the marketplace. If you have read up to this point, you no longer have the excuse of not knowing what to do because nobody has assigned you. Open your eyes. Step in where you see a need. Empty the trash cans when they are full, instead of adding your own trash to the already-spilling-over can. Grab the mop and dry up the spill on the break room floor. Be the extra set of hands in the children's church to facilitate their activities. Volunteer at the church office to make phone calls to all first-time visitors and pray with them. The list is endless. Blessed is the one who, when the Master returns, will be found doing (Luke 12:43). The problem with most people is the desire for recognition. Will you continue doing, even if no one recognizes your service?

Gideon was so tired of all the stories of miracles performed by Israel's God. His current reality did not suggest he belonged to a people who served a God that delivered. Israel had sinned against the Lord and had consequently fallen under the torment of the Midianites, the Amalekites, and the children of the East. Israel was greatly impoverished because the enemies would come in and destroy their crops and take away their cattle. Picture a flourishing land under siege for seven years, with enemy soldiers regularly raiding. The Israelites were miserable and in anguish, so much that they cried unto the Lord. Now Gideon decided to thresh wheat in a winepress, to hide it from the Midianites. That is a creative and innovative initiative! It is amazing what people can come up with in the midst of a crisis. Most people are more inspired and creative in stressful circumstances. They tend to discover a side of themselves they never knew existed. Gideon became creative in his search for survival. To ensure sustenance for his family, Gideon took the initiative to hide and thresh wheat where the enemy was least likely to look. He saw a problem and decided to become the solution. What have you done about the needs you see all around you? Do you focus on blame or fix the problem? Could it be that the need is staring you in the face because its assignment is to jump-start your innovative side? That situation that has the capability to ruffle your feathers may have a mission of awakening the dormant genius within you. Could it be that you were created to solve that problem that seems to pluck your last nerve?

Gideon questioned the angel of the Lord, expressing his frustrations when the angel told him that the Lord was with him:

> And Gideon said unto him, O my Lord, if the Lord be with us, why then is all this befallen us? And where be all his miracles which our fathers told us of, saying, Did not the Lord bring us up from Egypt? But now the Lord hath forsaken us and delivered us into the hands of the Midianites. (Judges 6:13)

He was the man God was looking for. He was innovative and creative enough to thresh wheat in the winepress; you bet he could take out the Midianites. His motivation was clear— his family's sustenance and his people's freedom. God just had to change his perspective and assure him that He would be with him:

> And the Lord said to him, "Surely I will be with thee, and thou shalt smite the Midianites as one man." (Judges 6:16)

Everything needed for you to fulfill your assignment is with you. All you need, to get moving, is the assurance of God's constant presence in that which you do. You see impoverished and penniless people all around you, and it drives you bonkers. You have all these ideas playing around in your head about how their lives could be better. What are you waiting for? Stop saying, "If only I had government grants, I would …" You can begin by sharing your genius ideas with these people, pull out the entrepreneur within them, change their mind-set regarding their current situation, and cause them to start seeing themselves as inherently better than their circumstance. That does not require a grant or money. A change of mind-set will bring about a change of status, even before the resources begin to come. You should start from somewhere, and the somewhere is within you. Gideon began defying the enemy by outwitting them before the rest of the provision came for the ultimate defeat of the Midianites. Provision always follows the vision. Have your vision in place; take the initiative to carry out aspects of it that can be done now; then watch and see what God does with it. All inventions are born out of a desire to solve a problem. Light shines brightest in the darkest of nights. Pressure has a way of pulling out the problem solver in you.

There must be a beating, shaking, and a crushing for the oil to flow out of the olives.

During David's fugitive oil-producing days, he found himself in the cave of Adullam. The Philistines had control of the land of Bethlehem. Something strange happened! David suddenly voiced a strong yearning that he had: "And David longed, and said, Oh that one would give me drink of the water of the well of Beth-lehem, which is by the gate" (2 Samuel 23:15). What an inconsiderate desire at a time like this! David was fully aware of the Philistine presence and garrison in Bethlehem. And he had the audacity to even think of wanting water only from the well of Bethlehem? He was quite specific about the location—the well by the gate. In David's defense, it was just a desire—wishful thinking, you might say, that happened to be verbalized in the vicinity of some of his men. Once they heard the yearning of the leader, these three mighty men of David took the initiative and went to work. David did not assign anyone to get him some water; he merely expressed a longing in his heart, and these men made it happen.

> And the three mighty men brake through the host of the Philistines, and drew water out of the well of Bethlehem, that was by the gate, and took it, and brought it to David: nevertheless, he would not drink thereof, but poured it out unto the LORD. (2 Samuel 23:16)

Do you have such loyal people working with you? Do you have individuals who believe in your cause to the point that they will do everything in their ability to propagate it? Do you have employees who genuinely believe in the vision of your company and will go the extra mile to serve the community in the furtherance of that vision? How many of your employees know your mission statement, vision, and goals? Does your church leadership team understand the vision and mandate of the ministry? It is an error to have in leadership positions, people who are not remotely interested in the vision of the organization. It is ideal to staff your organization with experts but even better to staff loyal experts. If you have to choose, settle for faithful people and then bring an expert to train them, rather than hiring experts with no interest in your vision.

It is worth noting that David's desire was not at all for the advantage of the people. It was totally for self-satisfaction, yet these men were determined to fulfill his wish. Are you a loyal employee? Are you committed to the vision of your organization? Do you execute the desires of leadership with zeal, or are you of the kind who questions every leadership decision and instigates others to do same? These men may have considered it a great privilege that they had an opportunity to hear the desire of David's heart. Many great leaders are so selfless and vision focused that they do not voice their personal needs and desires. Everything they say and do is geared toward the accomplishment of the vision. Sometimes, everyone goes with the flow, forgetting that these leaders are humans. Have you been privileged to notice a personal need in your pastor's life? Did you meet the need? Did you realize that God was giving you an opportunity to serve and take the initiative? If

God permits you to see their gas tank at E, do something about it. If you happen to hear the growling sounds of the deacon's stomach as he lays hands on you, do something about it after service. Please do something to meet the need without drama! Do not mobilize the entire congregation to raise funds because you "just can't stand seeing the pastor's children dressed like that one more day." If you cannot privately go shopping to meet the need, leave it alone and pray. Do not make your pastor a charity case without their knowledge. That is an insult to the dignity of God's servant. All giving that will attract God's reward must be done with respect for the dignity of the one receiving. Anything short of that is degrading and insulting to the God of provision who assigned you to give. Don't get me wrong. Funds can be raised for projects to be accomplished, as long as the motive is right and the actions involved are carried out with the right spirit. If you are going to donate toward a cause just so you can tell all your friends about your generosity, you might as well flush it down the toilet. You will not receive God's reward for it. The Outreach ministry of our organization carries out back-to-school drives annually in the summer, to assist families with school supplies. As minute as it may sound, lots of families come out to collect these free school supplies because those dollars add up pretty quickly. Many parents express the relief of not having to worry about school supplies for four kids. We have to caution and train our staff to treat them with dignity and respect when they come: we let them know that it is an honor for us to be of assistance, and we thank them for giving us access to be a blessing. We engage them in conversation, get to know them, and pray with those who may want prayers. We inform them about the variety of resources that the organization offers and how they can benefit from these resources with no strings attached. All of these we do with the help of our donors and members, who understand the power of hospitality God's way.

Is your presence making a difference in your company or church? A typical question asked at a job interview has to do with what you think you can bring into the company to improve it. When my husband and I started the church, we had to pick up and drop off church members, since many of them did not own cars. We would leave our home early on Sunday morning to make at least two trips, and then sometimes up to four trips after service (some people found rides to church, hoping someone from church would drop them off after service). All of that changed with the arrival of two new members. These two ladies sat down and mapped out routes according to zip codes of all the people who needed rides. They made a resolution that as long as they were around, their pastors would not be picking up and dropping off, unless they wanted to. They did not tell us their decision. We only found out later as we noticed that the people were taken care of. What a blessing that was to us! I will never forget the first Sunday that my husband and I were told that no one needed a ride and that we could go home. We had to just drive home from church—just the two of us! It felt very strange, but it blessed us. We were praising God and releasing blessings on those sisters, as we drove home. The gesture might look minute, but it was huge for us. They saw a need we never talked about, and they decided to be relevant in meeting that need. Today, the transportation ministry of the church has many more volunteer drivers, serving God by giving rides to God's precious people. Both ladies now serve in pastoral roles within the ministry, and are also involved in diverse missions work.

What can you do in your world that will reduce the workload of your leadership? Can you decide to learn how to play a musical instrument because there is a need for it at your church? I learned to play the drums because there was a need for a drummer. What initiative have you taken toward establishing an evangelism team for your church? Please do not say nobody listens to you. When you take charge by doing, those with similar passion will join you. Most movements began with one person.

I pleaded with my supervisor to train me in handling something outside of my job description (without demanding a pay raise), just to facilitate the productivity level of my work department. It served my company well, though some of my colleagues thought it was stupid of me to request additional work without extra pay. That skill set remained with me and now serves me well in the ministry. Have you checked to see if your skill set is needed at your church? Do you work as an accountant in a law firm, yet your church has no one to audit its books? How can you be a special education professional and the children workers at your church have no hands-on training in handling special needs kids? You could organize a free in-house training to equip the children workers. How about hosting a Health Awareness Day or Health Expo as a registered nurse? As a high school football coach, you can do something with the young people in your neighborhood to keep them out of trouble. Not everything is about money. Some gestures will pay you back in more ways than one. The look on the face of that single mother, with tears streaming down her cheeks, as she tells you how her son's grades have improved since he met you; the teenage girl who stops self-mutilating because you taught her to love herself by showing her love; the young lady who testifies about not aborting a pregnancy because you provided a support system for her; we can go on and on. These results in themselves are priceless and fulfilling. As a manager, supervisor, administrator, pastor, director, coach, class president, parent, family head, or whatever position of authority you may occupy, you can choose to positively impact and influence the people in your sphere. Instead of being arrogant, judgmental, and condescending, decide to be a mentor. Do not try to impress them but improve them. Do not kiss up to them, but help them clean up their mess (or at least show them how). Assist them in demystifying success, though not allowing them to remain mischievous. Let them know what your expectations are because you believe in their potential and skill set, assuring them that they have permission to make mistakes as they attempt to venture. Yes, you can also serve those under you, because service actually goes both ways. Take the initiative to know the state of your flock.

Be thou diligent to know the state of thy flocks, and look well to thy herds. (Proverbs 27:23 KJV)

Whenever you shepherd, know the faces of your sheep and set your heart upon your flock. (Proverbs 27:23 Aramaic Bible in Plain English)

Be diligent to know the countenance of thy cattle, and consider thy own flocks. (Proverbs 27:23 Douay-Rheims Bible)

Service is a two-way street. The scripture mentioned above says the one in a mentoring/shepherding/leadership role must serve by knowing the state/countenance/face of their flock (those under your guidance). It is impressive when the company's CEO knows the names of the janitors, mailman, pizza delivery guy, pastoral care personnel, cafeteria staff, gift shop cashier, and receptionists. I am not suggesting that you get to know all your employees and their children's birthdays in order to be a good leader, but some basic gestures reveal an interest in your employees. These are real people with real-life issues. Would you notice if your office manager came to work disturbed? You wouldn't unless you knew how she looked on a regular day. Are you so focused on your daily tasks that you give them instructions without even looking up from your desk into their faces? Are they just statistics to you? Is your patient just a diagnosis and room number? You will undoubtedly receive excellent service from the waiter whose name you remember to use. This is simply because your ability to recall and use his name (even though he has a name tag) suggests that you acknowledge and treat him as a person, not just a service. Try it sometime. The smallest things yield the greatest impact. In a conjugal setting, a woman's heart warms up to her husband when he seems to notice her favorite color, how she likes her coffee, and how she twitches when she is embarrassed. It says he is interested in her person. Serving with initiative should stir you up to know menial things about the one you are serving; this brings their person into focus.

In Nehemiah 2:1–2, King Artaxerxes noticed a change in the countenance of his cup bearer. He therefore inquired if all was well because he could tell that Nehemiah was sorrowful:

"Wherefore the king said unto me, why is thy countenance sad, seeing thou art not sick? This is nothing else but sorrow of heart" (Nehemiah 2:2).

The king was able to serve Nehemiah, through his giving, for the rebuilding of the walls of Jerusalem.

Joseph was able to notice the sad countenance of the butler and baker of Pharaoh because they both had disturbing dreams. When Joseph came to them in the morning and looked at them, he saw that they were sad and depressed. "So he asked pharaoh's officers who were in custody with him in his master's house, why do you look so dejected and sad today?" (Genesis 40:6–7 AMP).

Joseph's duty was to serve them (Genesis 40:4), not to get into their personal business, but he knew their faces and therefore noticed by looking at them that they were sad. How often do we regrettably comment (after an incident), "Come to think of it, the signs were all there, but I just did not see them"? Parents say it after the child has shot and killed his classmates and teacher; psychiatrists say it after the patient has drowned her kids in the bathtub. Wives say it after the husbands are strung out on drugs; children say it after their mom has overdosed on painkillers; pastors say it after the parishioner commits suicide; and on and on. Pay attention to people! Treat them as people and do not be passive with your service toward them. Be intentional about looking into the faces of the people around you and show interest. Do it in moderation, not stalking them or prying into their affairs in a snoopy manner but enough to know when they are troubled, disturbed, frantic, threatened, depressed, afraid, weirdly jumpy, and oddly different, as well as when excited, happy, and elated.

Mothers know that feeling they get when their baby is not looking right. They cannot put the finger on what the problem might be because they are not qualified to diagnose, but they just know. Health care workers have been known to take these complaints seriously because moms know their babies. They will run tests and sometimes keep the baby for further observation, even if everything seems okay on the surface. They trust the knowing of the mom because she observes her child daily and will quickly pick up on a wrong vibe before it becomes apparent. I think it is also a nurturing instinct predominantly in women. Most husbands will tell you that they have learned (the hard way, most often) to listen to their wives. At first, it sounds stupid and petty when she says, "I don't know, but something about your friend Jim seems odd," or "The deal looks good, and the contract seems fair, but something doesn't feel right." Most men, being rational rather than emotional beings, would say, "That does not make any sense. You are paranoid. You are just negative and controlling." They go ahead with the decision, and then disaster strikes. A word of advice for you ladies: never say (or give them a look that says), "I told you so."

Countless disasters and catastrophes have been averted due to early detection by keen and engaging eyes: rape victims saved, kidnapped kids rescued, home invasion stopped, bank robbery busted, blackmailed employee vindicated, suicide attempt interrupted, battered women rescued, post-partum depression controlled, and more. No matter your position in life, whether at the top or at the bottom or somewhere in between, you are called to serve. Offer to help before you are asked. Remember, diligently serving in these small things indicates that you are qualified for big things. Joseph served his brothers in the field, in Potiphar's house, and in jail. These all got him ready for the Pharaoh's palace. If you are too big to initiate acts of service, you are too small to lead initiatives!

8 Serving with Respect for Protocol

Every home, relationship, school, church, ministry, company, organization, nation, and people group has a code of conduct. This code of conduct could be written or verbally handed down or both. The institutions mentioned above (careful choice of the word) have a gate or entrance point through which you access them without any qualms. But there is a problem: this gate is invisible. This explains why you can live in a house but not access the home. A woman may be married to a man but has no access to his heart. A child can go through an educational system and obtain a degree without getting the education. A man works for a company for thirty years yet did not access the vision. A man is happily married for ten years but cannot penetrate his wife's family. A young man gets his father's inheritance but fails to access his wealth; people go to church but fail to access the anointing available to lift burdens and destroy yokes; you serve under a man or woman of God and obtain an ordination certificate without access to the mantle they carry. These things ought not to be so, but people perish for lack of knowledge. There is an invisible gate into every institution. We must of necessity walk in the conscious awareness of its existence. Lacking knowledge of this truth does not diminish its presence; it simply makes you stagger and grope in a dark maze for years, while the gate is hidden in plain sight. There is a code to access this invisible gate: it is the code of conduct; it is its protocol.

✓ Protocol has nothing to do with wrong or right; it has everything to do with an acceptable, existing, and established way of life within a particular institution, realm, or environment. Success will not be attained by anyone who does not follow, from a place of honor, the protocol of achievement. When you choose to enter that environment, it becomes your prerogative to study the protocol in order to gain access. Some protocols are nicely written down and filed away in company manuals: a company's rules on staffing, hazardous waste disposal, fire, communication, conflict resolution, and so on. Some are summarized, laminated, and posted on hallway bulletin boards, above-the- door ledges, elevators, and restroom mirrors (depending on the content and severity). Some are verbally handed down (dress code for a birthday party, for example). Others appear at the bottom of a brochure you are given at the wedding, graduation, church service, or funeral program. Some are nonverbal and nonwritten; that means, you figure it out! So, pay attention:

✓ You want to get into an institution.

✓ It has an invisible gate.

✓ The gate has a code that will grant you access (protocol).

✓ It may be written, verbally communicated, or a puzzle for you to solve.

✓ You must gain access to this institution because the benefits are enormous.

✓ Quitting is not an option; getting frustrated will not help; being in a hurry may be of no use; being arrogant and self-promoting is not a good idea; pushing and throwing weighty names may not cut it.

✓ You must assess the environment for clues into the protocol of that institution and respectfully follow it, even if it defies your logic.

Service is the key to influence, and you must gain access in order to serve in an impactful way. Access must be given, never seized. You can call a mandatory staff meeting in which you lecture for hours but fail to get through to your staff members because even though they are physically present, they are actually absent. You cannot usurp access; it must be given. People give you access when you show honor and respect for their existing protocol. We know we are the salt of the earth and the light of the world, but our saltiness and illumination are not felt or seen in certain circles because we lack respect for protocol necessary to access that milieu. I will never forget an experience I had on October 10, 2013. We had been praying that God would make us relevant to our community, as a ministry, and He had been faithful in giving us instructions to follow. On this remarkable day, I had a waking dream, and at exactly

04:45 a.m., I suddenly sat up in bed with these words coming out of my mouth: "If you want legal grounds to comment on someone's message, you must get in beyond the iron curtain." I pondered on that information, praying in tongues and listening in for an explanation from God. The Spirit of God spoke these words to me in prayer: "You must be given access to affect and influence. There is an invisible gate through which you must pass, and the key to accessing the other side of that iron curtain is your honor for existing protocol." This revelation caused a shift in my being and has significantly shifted things in our ministry. Praise God!

Jesus was given access to read the Word in the synagogue, though He was and is the Word (Luke 4:17). When He was done reading, He closed the book, gave it back to the minister, and sat down (Luke 4:20). Do you greet the people as asked and return the microphone or do you preach the sermon too? Do you come up to give a testimony but end up singing a song before the testimony? Jesus knew the importance of proper representation as it pertains to access. That is why He schooled the disciples on respect for protocol before releasing them to the towns and villages where He would later go (Luke 10:1–10). He knew that if they misrepresented Him in any way, the invisible iron gate would be shut to Him. Does your conduct close the door to the Gospel? Many born-again believers are such poor representatives of the Gospel in the workplace. We are known for tardiness and inconsistencies. It breaks my heart to hear Christians say they will never hire anyone who says they are Christian. We are seemingly known to be the most undisciplined set of people, under the guise of the Spirit's leadings. Let the real Christians arise and change this narrative, please!

Do your homework about a people group before attempting to penetrate them with the Gospel. What may be socially or culturally acceptable to you may be repulsive and disrespectful to them. Show some respect! I am not in any way suggesting that you get into demonic practices of a people group to gain access. Paul said, "I have become all things to all people so that by all possible means I might gain some" (1 Corinthians 9:22 NLT). He was not referring to compromising with sin but rather dealing with the mode of life that neither hurts nor enhances the Gospel directly, except for how it is applied. If you have to veil yourself to access a particular institution as a woman, for example, so be it. Wearing a veil or not wearing a veil does not directly affect the standard of God's Word because either option is not a sin. However, your decision to cover yourself when penetrating a people group that values it will enhance your effectiveness in reaching the people because they will open up to you more. Most people tend to see you before they hear you, though it is not always a fair assessment of character. That is how you gain access by honoring existing protocol.

Avoid behavior that suggests superiority. Appreciate the bamboo bed the same as you would a Sleep Number bed at a five-star hotel. Eat whatever is given to you with thanksgiving (Luke 10:8). Eating with them and eating their food the way they eat it (at least attempting to) will open doors. In Acts 16:14–15, we are told that God opened Lydia's heart to attend to Paul's preaching. She later constrained them to lodge in her house. Paul requested prayers for doors to be open for the Gospel message to be received (Colossians 4:3). He talks about how they have labored in the work in such a way as not to put an obstruction in anyone's path, so that the ministry is not blamed (2 Corinthians 6:3).

Access can be lost if abused. If someone welcomes you into their home and tells you to feel at home, they are by no means suggesting that you take your shoes off and place your feet on their coffee table, drink their milk straight out of the gallon, and walk around in your underwear—if that's what you do at home. Familiarity causes a lot of people to abuse access, and they only later on discover that the once-open gate has been shut in their faces.

- ✓ Respect people's personal space and do not assume what people mean when they speak. Ask questions for clarity and understanding.
- ✓ Respect the privacy and dignity of people; learn to take the microphone away from your mouth as you minister sensitive things to people on a one-on-one basis.
- ✓ Apologize quickly when you recognize a misunderstanding or miscommunication. Follow peace with all people.
- ✓ Watch against becoming territorial and possessive, recognizing that others will equally gain access when they use the right key. Don't be like the elder brother of the prodigal son in Luke 15:11–32.

✓ Receive correction and grow, no matter where, when, and how it comes.

✓ Refuse to participate in demeaning conversations about others. Be a builder.

✓ Avoid self-promoting discussions; be quick to hear and slow to speak. You won't know who you are sitting next to if you are the only one talking. You can learn a thing or two if you can get yourself to shut up. Discern difference and recognize greatness.

✓ You will serve better if you stay vigilant. Read the signs! Literally!

✓ Never stop learning. How long you sit determines how high you soar when you rise.

If you think you are too superior to submit to the protocol of an institution (church, company, home, nation, people group), you will quickly find out that you are way too inferior to impact it. If you are too big for protocol, you are too small for impact and influence. Too big for small things, too small for big things!

Conclusion

Grow Up! It's a Choice

Arise, body of Christ, and shine. Your salvation is nearer now than when you first believed (Romans 13:11). We do not have much time left before the return of Jesus our King. We ought, therefore, to walk circumspectly, not as fools but as wise, redeeming the time (Ephesians 5:14–19). Refuse to be drunk with wine or to be occupied with intellectual debates about drinking; rather, be filled with the Holy Ghost and do exploits for God. Offer your body as a living sacrifice, holy, acceptable, and pleasing to God, which is your reasonable service (Romans 12:1). God has blessed us with all spiritual blessings in heavenly places in Christ and has given us all things that pertain unto life and godliness (Ephesians 1:3; 2 Peter 1:3). These blessings will only manifest in us through the knowledge of Him who has called us to glory and virtue. It is time to grow up in the knowledge and grace of Jesus Christ.

> For when for the time ye ought to be teachers, ye have need that one teach you again which be the first principles of the oracles of God; and are become such as have need of milk, and not

of strong meat. For every one that useth milk is unskillful in the word of righteousness: for he is a babe. But strong meat belongeth to them that are of full age, even those who by reason of use have their senses exercised to discern both good and evil. (Hebrews 5:12–14)

If you have read up to this point, I congratulate you, because it shows your desire for growth and reveals your level of maturity. Strong meat is not for babies. It is for those who are of full age. Your maturity level can be measured by your level of self-control. Everyone has equal opportunities to be governed by the flesh, but the mature person puts their flesh under subjection (1 Corinthians 9:25, 27) and decides with the help of the Holy Spirit to walk in the Spirit (Galatians 5:16, 25). The child is not very different from the servants, though he is the heir and master of all; he is kept under tutors until he becomes a mature son (Galatians 4:1). It is time for you to arise, grow up, and take your place. It is time to take hold of our Father's estate and execute His will with precision. 1 Corinthians 14:20 says in the Amplified version: "Continue to be babies in (matters of) evil, but in your minds be mature (men)." You may consider this insulting because you claim to be grown. I do not intend to offend you but to bring to your awareness the truth of God's Word without adulterating its intent. We must walk in the fullness of God's power before Jesus returns. We must separate ourselves from all superfluity of naughtiness, embrace the engrafted word, and work it out

(James 1:21–25). Mysteries of the kingdom are available to us if we can handle them. Jesus told his disciples in John 16:12 that he had much to say to them, but they were not equipped to handle it. The Holy Spirit was the one to come and equip them and reveal much more to them. Now we have the Holy Spirit. What's our excuse? Paul echoes the words of Jesus in his dealings with the Corinthian church:

> And I, brethren, could not speak unto you as unto spiritual, but as unto carnal, even as unto babes in Christ.

> I have fed you with milk, and not with meat: for hitherto ye were not able to bear it, neither yet now are ye able. (1 Corinthians 3:1–2 KJV)

If your supervisor is extra careful in correcting you because you are very tender and the rest of your workday will be messed up, you are a baby. Grow up! Do you give people permission to disagree with you without you disliking them? Can you handle rebuke and take criticism without throwing a tantrum like a three-year-old? Do you still stamp your feet and slam doors when things do not go your way? Paul explains to them why he calls them carnal and childish. He describes carnality and the lack of spirituality as follows: envy, strife, and division. If you are a quarrelsome person, who constantly sows discord and promotes cliques and factions, you are carnal, childish, and unspiritual. Some adults will forbid other adults from having conversations with certain people, just because they do not like them. What a level of childishness! We are no more in middle school, folks, where we used to alienate the girl with the fancy clothes because of our jealousy—until she became insecure and gave us her lunch money just to belong to our clique.

Many in the body of Christ have left the preaching of God's Word and are now using their pulpits as the platform to settle scores with their opponents. We cannot afford to handle God's Word in craftiness and deceit but in sincerity and truth (1 Corinthians 5:8; 2 Corinthians 4:1–2; Romans 1:18). How dare you use the pulpit to attack another ministry or minister? God is not picking sides between you and the other preacher; you both are His sons. The devil has successfully distracted us, making us focus our energy on fighting one another, while he is busy plundering the earth for hell. Who made you a judge over another person's servant? If your brother is overtaken in a fault, the Bible admonishes that you who are spiritual should restore that brother in the spirit of meekness. If you cannot do that, pray for that person and keep your mouth shut (Galatians 6:1). Intercessors shut their mouths before people and open them before God! We are all laborers in God's vineyard, and we need all hands on deck in this final hour to bring in the end-time harvest. Instead of serving grudgingly, competitively, and with no sense of direction or purpose, why not focus on your assignment and pray for those who seem to be off track? God, who is the Master of us all, has the ability to restore and redirect His servant-son. You must be grateful to the Lord for keeping you consistent in Him because it is His grace at work within you (Philippians 2:13). Do not take credit for the work of salvation in your life. Refuse to walk in carnality, because the carnal man cannot receive or know the things of God (1 Corinthians 2:14).

Grow in Love (1 Corinthians 13)

Speaking of love as a manifestation of maturity, Paul insinuates that not walking in love is proof of childishness:

> When I was a child, I spake as a child, I understood as a child, I thought as a child: but when I became a man, I put away childish things.

> Put away the childishness of envy, strife, and factions, and become a man in understanding. (1 Corinthians 13:11)

> Owe no man any thing, but to love one another: for he that loveth another hath fulfilled the law. (Romans 13:8 KJV)

> Love worketh no ill to his neighbour: therefore love is the fulfilling of the law.

> And that, knowing the time, that now it is high time to awake out of sleep: for now is our salvation nearer than when we believed.

> The night is far spent, the day is at hand: let us therefore cast off the works of darkness, and let us put on the armour of light.

Let us walk honestly, as in the day; not in rioting and drunkenness, not in chambering and wantonness, not in strife and envying.

But put ye on the Lord Jesus Christ, and make not provision for the flesh, to fulfil the lusts thereof. (Romans 13:10–14 KJV)

Do you get where I am going with this? The entire chapter speaks about order and submission in love, which can only be practiced by mature people, not babies. Then he warns about the urgent need for growth and maturity because we do not have the time to be running around in diapers with a feeding bottle in hand, crying about our hurt feelings; meanwhile, we are supposed to be living in the Spirit.

Grow in Grace (2 Peter 1:2)

Decide to be committed to your own victory by marrying the Word of God. Grow in grace through the knowledge of the Word. Choose to study God's Word to show yourself approved unto God, not unto man (2 Timothy 2:15). There is a difference between reading and studying. Studying the Word for preaching purposes only is studying done to be approved by humans. You are first a child of God, before you are a preacher. Discipline yourself to study the Word to be fed and equipped; then preaching and teaching will be a spontaneous overflow from your times with God. The grace of God does not condone sin but rather teaches us to deny ungodliness (Titus 2:11–12).

Grow in Your Assignment and Get Busy (John 9:4)

People who know their identity tend to celebrate difference in others rather than compete with them. They know and understand that difference does not translate to opposition but as variety and diversity. They complement rather than compete. Babies react to everything with crying and tantrums; grown folks process and respond to situations through the light of the Word. Be the grown-up. Babies are thermometers, while grown-ups are thermostats. Be the grown-up. Set the tone rather than analyze and report the current temperature. If what you see is not a reflection of God's standard, change it on your knees, following the guidelines of the Word. We have no right to complain about anything if we have not yet done everything scripturally permissible to change it.

Grow in Humility (James 4:6–17)

Humble yourself and live on purpose. Serve every day in every way, as unto the Lord. Always be open to learning from anyone. As long as it is the Word, receive it, no matter the delivery and the vessel used to deliver it. God resists the proud but gives grace to the humble. The depth of your humility and submission to God determines the strength of your resistance against darkness. You will revenge all disobedience when your obedience is fulfilled (2 Corinthians 10:6). Staying under authority puts you in authority over all opposition of the wicked. If you are too big for submission, you are too small for dominion.

Grow in Your Quest for Wisdom (Proverbs 4:7)

Refuse the know-it-all attitude. When you stop learning, you stop growing. Wisdom is the principal thing. Never minimize wisdom. Seek it consistently, and you will not miss its opportunities, no matter its disguises. Solving the problems you encounter and overcoming the obstacles will produce growth in wisdom. Learn from the experiences of others. When the sons of the widow announced that there were no more vessels, the oil stopped flowing (2 Kings 4:6). If you are too big to pursue wisdom, you are too small to be pursued by wealth!

If you are too big for these small things, you are definitely too small for the big things God has in store for you!

Printed in the United States
by Baker & Taylor Publisher Services